CW00499417

The Ultimate Tower 2-Basket Air Fryer Cookbook UK

2000 Days of Super Tasty and Hot Air Fryer Meals for Beginners to Satisfy Your Family's Favorites (using UK measurements)

Jane R. Conner

Copyright© 2024 By Jane R. Conner
All Rights Reserved

This book is copyright protected. It is only for personal use.
You cannot amend, distribute, sell, use,
quote or paraphrase any part of the content within this book,
without the consent of the author or publisher.
Under no circumstances will any blame or
legal responsibility be held against the publisher,
or author, for any damages, reparation,
or monetary loss due to the information contained within this book,
either directly or indirectly.

Disclaimer Notice:
Please note the information contained within this
document is for educational and entertainment purposes only.
All effort has been executed to present accurate,
up to date, reliable, complete information.
No warranties of any kind are declared or implied.
Readers acknowledge that the author is not engaged
in the rendering of legal,
financial, medical or professional advice.
The content within this book has been derived from various sources.
Please consult a licensed professional before attempting any
techniques outlined in this book.
By reading this document,
the reader agrees that under no circumstances is the
author responsible for any losses,
direct or indirect,
that are incurred as a result of the use of the
information contained within this document, including,
but not limited to, errors, omissions, or inaccuracies.

Contents

INTRODUCTION

Unleashing Culinary Magic: The Tower Dual Basket Air Fryer

• 1. What is a Tower Dual Basket Air Fryer?

In the symphony of kitchen appliances, the Tower Dual Basket Air Fryer emerges as a virtuoso, weaving together innovation and culinary prowess. Imagine a sleek, compact powerhouse sitting on your countertop, beckoning you to reimagine the way you cook. This is no ordinary kitchen companion; this is the maestro of air frying – the Tower Dual Basket Air Fryer.

At its essence, this culinary wizard is a contraption that defies convention. It's not just an air fryer; it's a dual-basket marvel, a kitchen prodigy that whispers promises of healthier indulgences and gastronomic adventures. The Tower Dual Basket Air Fryer is a testament to the marriage of cutting-edge technology and culinary artistry.

The Features and Benefits of Tower Dual Basket

• Dual-Basket Enchantment:

The pièce de résistance, the dual-basket functionality of the Tower Air Fryer, elevates it to a realm where culinary dreams come true. No longer confined to a singular gastronomic endeavor, you can orchestrate a culinary symphony, cooking two distinct dishes simultaneously. Picture this: golden fries sizzling in one basket while succulent chicken wings crisp up in the other. It's a culinary ballet, a duet of flavors, and it's happening right on your countertop.

• Rapid Air Technology:

Step into the future of cooking with the Tower Dual Basket Air Fryer's crown jewel – rapid air technology. As the appliance breathes life into hot air, it dances around your food, cocooning it in a cyclone of heat. This isn't just cooking; it's a transformative experience. The result? A tantalizingly crispy exterior that conceals a world of succulence within. Say goodbye to the greasy guilt of traditional frying and embrace the crisp embrace of innovation.

• Adjustable Temperature Mastery:

Cooking is an art, and the Tower Dual Basket Air Fryer hands you the palette. With an adjustable temperature range, you become the maestro, conducting the heat to your culinary desires. Whether it's a gentle bake or a bold sear, the power is in your hands. This isn't just an appliance; it's an

extension of your culinary creativity.

• **Digital Timer Serenade:**

In the realm of gastronomy, timing is everything. The Tower Dual Basket Air Fryer knows this, and it serenades you with a digital timer. Watch the digits dance as your creations come to life. Precision meets simplicity, ensuring that your culinary masterpieces are orchestrated to perfection, every single time.

• **Easy-to-Clean Choreography:**

The kitchen is your stage, and the Tower Dual Basket Air Fryer believes in a seamless performance. Cleaning becomes a choreography, a dance of dismantling and reassembling. The removable parts, often blessed with dishwasher-safe grace, make the after-party cleanup a breeze. It's not just about the cooking; it's about the entire culinary experience, from prep to the joyous aftermath.

• **Versatile Culinary Odyssey:**

The Tower Dual Basket Air Fryer isn't content with a singular act; it craves variety. Frying, baking, roasting, grilling – it's a versatile virtuoso. From morning delights to evening feasts, this appliance transforms your kitchen into a realm of endless possibilities. It's not just about cooking; it's about embarking on a culinary odyssey, exploring flavors and cuisines with boundless enthusiasm.

• **Healthier Indulgences:**

Tradition whispers tales of deep-fried delights, but the Tower Dual Basket Air Fryer redefines the narrative. It's a champion of healthier indulgences, allowing you to relish the crispy goodness without drowning your creations in a sea of oil. Feel the guilt dissipate as you savor guilt-free pleasures, courtesy of this culinary maverick.

• **Time-Saving Symphony:**

In a world where time is the elusive maestro, the Tower Dual Basket Air Fryer orchestrates a time-saving symphony. Simultaneous cooking means your culinary creations emerge together, a harmonious ensemble ready to be savored. Weeknight dinners become a breeze, and entertaining guests becomes a seamless performance. Time bends to your culinary will.

• **Energy-Efficient Performance:**

The Tower Dual Basket Air Fryer isn't just a culinary powerhouse; it's an environmental ally. With its efficient heating mechanism and abbreviated cooking times, it's a nod to energy-conscious cooking. As you revel in your gastronomic creations, you can also relish the fact that you're making eco-friendly choices.

How to Use Tower Dual Basket Air Fryer: Tips for Culinary Success

Here's your guide to unlocking the full potential of the dual baskets and transforming your kitchen into a haven of gastronomic delight.

• Dual Basket Dance:

Embrace the unique dance of the dual baskets. Seize the opportunity to cook two distinct dishes simultaneously. Whether it's crispy fries paired with succulent chicken wings or delicate pastries dancing alongside savory skewers, the dual basket feature is your culinary pas de deux.

• Temperature Tango:

Become the maestro of your kitchen with the adjustable temperature control. Different foods demand different temperatures. From the gentle warmth needed for baked treats to the fiery intensity required for a perfect sear, the Tower Dual Basket Air Fryer puts you in control. Let your culinary creations dance to the rhythm of customized heat.

• Timing Waltz:

Precision meets performance with the digital timer. Imagine your culinary creations waltzing to the perfect doneness, orchestrated by the timely countdown. No more guesswork – just flawless culinary choreography. Set the timer, sit back, and watch your dishes perform a culinary waltz of perfection.

• Marination Foxtrot:

Before the dual baskets take center stage, indulge in the marination foxtrot. Infuse your ingredients with flavor, allowing them to tango with spices and herbs. The Tower Dual Basket Air Fryer is not just a cook; it's a partner in enhancing flavors. Let the foxtrot of marination set the stage for a tantalizing performance.

• Layering Ballet:

In the Tower Dual Basket Air Fryer, every dish is a layered ballet. Consider the arrangement of ingredients as a choreography of taste. Place heartier items at the bottom basket, ensuring they absorb the full impact of the hot air. Delicate treats pirouette in the top basket, soaking in the nuances of the culinary performance.

• Shake and Savor Samba

Midway through the cooking extravaganza, engage in the shake and savor samba. Gently shake the baskets to ensure an even coating of

crispiness. It's not just about cooking; it's about actively participating in the culinary spectacle. This simple move ensures that every bite is a flavorful revelation.

• Culinary Creativity Rhapsody

The Tower Dual Basket Air Fryer isn't just an appliance; it's a canvas for your culinary creativity. Break free from conventional recipes and embark on a rhapsody of flavors. Experiment with ingredients, spices, and textures. Let your imagination compose a culinary symphony that tantalizes the taste buds and leaves a lasting impression.

• Resting Interlude:

As your culinary creations emerge, allow them a resting interlude. Like performers after a captivating show, your dishes need a moment to settle. This interlude ensures that the flavors harmonize, reaching a crescendo of taste that will leave you and your guests in awe.

How to Clean Tower Dual Basket Air Fryer

• Post-Culinary Serenity:

The culinary journey is exhilarating, but the post-culinary serenity begins with the art of cleaning. As the final notes of the culinary symphony fade, enter the Zen of maintenance. Cleaning the Tower Dual Basket Air Fryer is not a chore; it's a meditative experience, a cleansing ritual to prepare for the next gastronomic adventure.

• Cool Down Prelude:

Before embarking on the cleaning odyssey, let the Tower Dual Basket Air Fryer cool down. This prelude is crucial for safety and ensures that you approach the cleaning process with a calm and collected mindset. Allow the appliance to cool, and let the culinary energy dissipate.

• Disassembly Sonata:

The Tower Dual Basket Air Fryer invites you to perform the disassembly sonata. Gently disassemble the components – the baskets, trays, and any removable parts. Each piece is a note in the cleaning symphony, contributing to the overall cleanliness and maintenance of the appliance.

• Dishwasher Harmony:

Blessed with dishwasher-safe components, the Tower Dual Basket Air Fryer simplifies the cleaning melody. Allow these components to dance in the dishwasher, harmonizing with the soapy serenade. It's not just about cleaning; it's about letting the dishwasher do the heavy lifting while you bask in the afterglow of culinary success.

• **Handwash Ballet:**

For those delicate components that prefer a handwash ballet, indulge them in a gentle rinse. Immerse them in warm, soapy water and let the water pirouette away any lingering residues. The handwash ballet is a tactile connection with your culinary companion, ensuring that every part is treated with care.

• **Exterior Elegance:**

The exterior of the Tower Dual Basket Air Fryer demands an elegance routine. Wipe it down with a soft, damp cloth, ensuring that every inch gleams with post-culinary radiance. This step is not just about cleanliness; it's about presenting a kitchen centerpiece that reflects your commitment to culinary excellence.

• **Filter Resonance:**

Let the filter resonance be heard. The Tower Dual Basket Air Fryer often comes equipped with filters to capture odors and grease. These filters, akin to a purifying melody, need attention. Depending on the model, they can be either replaceable or washable. Ensure their performance remains harmonious by following the manufacturer's guidance.

• **Storage Coda:**

As the cleaning symphony reaches its crescendo, prepare for the storage coda. Allow all components to dry thoroughly before reassembling the Tower Dual Basket Air Fryer. Store it with the grace of a final bow, knowing that it's ready for an encore – another culinary performance that awaits.

• **Regular Maintenance Sonata:**

Embrace the regular maintenance sonata as a routine. Regular cleaning ensures that your Tower Dual Basket Air Fryer remains a pristine canvas for your culinary creations. Like a well-tuned instrument, this appliance performs at its best when cared for regularly.

• **Epilogue: A Culinary Sonata**

In the realm of kitchen appliances, the Tower Dual Basket Air Fryer is not just an instrument; it's a maestro orchestrating a culinary sonata. From mastering the dual baskets to embracing the Zen of maintenance, your journey with this appliance transcends the ordinary. As you embark on each culinary adventure, remember that every note, every tip, and every cleaning step is a harmonious contribution to the culinary symphony you create. The Tower Dual Basket Air Fryer is not just a tool; it's a companion in your

FAQ about Tower Dual Basket Air Fryer

• Q1: What makes the Tower Dual Basket Air Fryer stand out from other air fryers?

The Tower Dual Basket Air Fryer distinguishes itself with its dual-basket functionality. This unique feature allows users to simultaneously cook two different dishes, offering unparalleled versatility in the kitchen. This sets it apart, making it a go-to appliance for those seeking efficiency and variety in their cooking.

• Q2: How does the dual-basket feature work, and what are its advantages?

The dual-basket feature allows users to cook two separate dishes at the same time. Each basket operates independently, ensuring that flavors do not intermingle. This not only saves time but also enhances the overall cooking experience by providing flexibility and convenience for preparing diverse meals simultaneously.

• Q3: Can I cook different types of food in each basket?

Absolutely! The dual-basket design is perfect for cooking different types of food simultaneously. For instance, you can have crispy fries in one basket while preparing a succulent piece of salmon in the other. It's a fantastic way to create balanced and varied meals without the need for multiple cooking sessions.

• Q4: How does the rapid air technology contribute to cooking in the Tower Dual Basket Air Fryer?

Rapid air technology is the culinary magic behind the Tower Dual Basket Air Fryer. It involves circulating hot air at high speed around the food, creating a crispy outer layer while preserving moisture inside. This not only ensures efficient and even cooking but also results in dishes that are delightfully crispy without the need for excessive oil.

• Q5: What temperature range does the Tower Dual Basket Air Fryer offer?

The Tower Dual Basket Air Fryer provides a customizable temperature range, giving users precise control over the cooking process. The adjustable temperature settings accommodate various recipes, allowing for gentle baking at lower temperatures and intense searing at higher temperatures.

• **Q6: How do I ensure that my food is cooked evenly in both baskets?**

To achieve even cooking in both baskets, consider the placement of items based on their cooking times and requirements. Additionally, engage in a gentle shake or rearrange the contents midway through the cooking process. This ensures that each piece receives equal exposure to the hot air, resulting in uniformly cooked and delicious dishes.

• **Q7: What are some tips for maximizing cooking success with the Tower Dual Basket Air Fryer?**

Preheat the Air Fryer: Allow the air fryer to preheat before placing food inside for more consistent results.

Mindful Marination: Enhance flavors by marinating ingredients before cooking.

Optimal Basket Loading: Distribute food evenly in the baskets, avoiding overcrowding for better air circulation.

Shake It Up: Give the baskets a gentle shake during cooking to ensure even crispiness.

Use a Meat Thermometer: For meats, use a thermometer to ensure they reach the desired internal temperature.

• **Q8: How do I clean the Tower Dual Basket Air Fryer effectively?**

Cool Down: Allow the air fryer to cool down before cleaning.

Disassemble Components: Gently disassemble removable components such as baskets and trays.

Dishwasher-Friendly: Many parts are dishwasher-safe; utilize this feature for easy cleaning.

Handwash Delicate Parts: Handwash delicate components using warm, soapy water.

Exterior Wipe Down: Wipe the exterior with a damp cloth for a clean finish.

Regular Maintenance: Make cleaning a routine for optimal performance.

• **Q9: Can I cook frozen food directly in the Tower Dual Basket Air Fryer?**

Yes, you can! The Tower Dual Basket Air Fryer excels at cooking frozen foods. Simply adjust the cooking time and temperature settings based on the specific item you are preparing, and enjoy the convenience of crisp and delicious frozen treats.

• **Q10: Is the Tower Dual Basket Air Fryer energy-efficient?**

Yes, the Tower Dual Basket Air Fryer is designed with energy efficiency in mind. Its rapid air technology and shorter cooking times contribute to energy savings compared to traditional cooking methods. Enjoy culinary delights while being mindful of your energy consumption.

In essence, the Tower Dual Basket Air Fryer is not just an appliance; it's a culinary companion that offers a unique cooking experience, efficiency, and versatility. With its dual-basket charm and innovative features, it invites users to explore the art of cooking in a whole new dimension.

Breakfast

Black Pudding Stuffed Mushrooms

Prep Time: 15 minutes / Cook Time: 20 minutes / Servings: 4 / Mode: Air Fry

Ingredients:

- 12 large mushrooms, cleaned and stems removed
- Salt and pepper to taste
- Fresh parsley for garnish (optional)
- 15ml olive oil
- 200g black pudding, crumbled

Preparation Instructions:

1. Preheat the Tower Dual Basket Air Fryer to 375°F in Air Fry mode.
2. In a bowl, mix crumbled black pudding with olive oil, salt, and pepper.
3. Stuff each mushroom cap with the black pudding mixture.
4. Arrange stuffed mushrooms in the air fryer basket, ensuring they are not touching.
5. Air fry for about 20 minutes, until mushrooms are tender and the filling is cooked.
6. Garnish with fresh parsley if desired, and serve hot.

Pumpkin Spice Latte Muffins

Prep Time: 15 minutes / Cook Time: 25 minutes / Servings: 12 / Mode: Bake

Ingredients:

- 220g all-purpose flour
- 5g baking powder
- 2.5g pumpkin pie spice
- 120ml strong brewed coffee, cooled
- 100g sugar
- 5g baking soda
- 120g pumpkin puree
- 50g brown sugar, packed
- 2.5g salt
- 5ml vanilla extract
- 60ml vegetable oil

Preparation Instructions:

1. Preheat the Tower Dual Basket Air Fryer to 350°F in Bake mode.
2. In a large bowl, whisk together flour, sugar, brown sugar, baking powder, baking soda, salt, and pumpkin pie spice.
3. In another bowl, mix pumpkin puree, brewed coffee, vegetable oil, and vanilla extract.
4. Combine wet and dry ingredients, stirring until just combined.
5. Line muffin cups with liners and fill each two-thirds full with the batter.
6. Bake in the air fryer for about 25 minutes or until a toothpick inserted comes out clean.
7. Allow muffins to cool before serving.

Lemon-Poppy Seed Scones

Prep Time: 15 minutes / Cook Time: 20 minutes / Servings: 6 / Mode: Bake

Ingredients:

- 250g all-purpose flour
- 1/4 teaspoon salt
- 1 tablespoon poppy seeds
- 5ml vanilla extract
- 50g sugar
- 120g cold unsalted butter, cubed
- 120ml milk
- 10g baking powder
- Zest of 1 lemon
- 1 large egg

Preparation Instructions:

1. Preheat the Tower Dual Basket Air Fryer to 375°F in Bake mode.
2. In a large bowl, combine flour, sugar, baking powder, and salt.

3. Add cold butter, lemon zest, and poppy seeds; mix until it resembles coarse crumbs.
4. In a separate bowl, whisk together milk, egg, and vanilla extract.
5. Pour wet ingredients into the dry mixture, stirring until just combined.
6. Turn dough onto a floured surface, pat into a circle, and cut into wedges.
7. Place scones on the air fryer basket, leaving space between each.
8. Air fry for about 20 minutes until golden brown.
9. Let cool slightly before serving.

Cranberry and Stilton Pancakes

Prep Time: 10 minutes / Cook Time: 15 minutes / Servings: 4 / Mode: Roast

Ingredients:
- 200g all-purpose flour
- 1 egg
- 100g dried cranberries
- 2 teaspoons baking powder
- 300ml milk
- Butter for greasing
- 1/2 teaspoon salt
- 50g Stilton cheese, crumbled

Preparation Instructions:
1. Preheat the Tower Dual Basket Air Fryer to 400°F in Roast mode.
2. In a bowl, whisk together flour, baking powder, and salt.
3. In another bowl, beat the egg and then stir in the milk.
4. Pour the wet ingredients into the dry ingredients, mixing until just combined.
5. Gently fold in Stilton cheese and dried cranberries.
6. Grease the air fryer basket with butter.
7. Spoon batter onto the basket to form pancakes.
8. Roast for about 15 minutes until the edges are golden.
9. Serve hot.

Marmite-Infused Avocado Toast

Prep Time: 10 minutes / Cook Time: 5 minutes / Servings: 2 / Mode: Air Fry

Ingredients:
- 2 slices whole-grain bread
- Salt and pepper to taste
- 1 ripe avocado, mashed
- Red pepper flakes for garnish (optional)
- 1 teaspoon Marmite

Preparation Instructions:
1. Preheat the Tower Dual Basket Air Fryer to 375°F in Air Fry mode.
2. Toast the slices of whole-grain bread until golden brown.
3. In a bowl, mix mashed avocado with Marmite, salt, and pepper.
4. Spread the Marmite-infused avocado evenly on the toasted bread slices.
5. Place the prepared toast in the air fryer basket.
6. Air fry for about 5 minutes until the edges are crisp.
7. Garnish with red pepper flakes if desired.
8. Serve hot and enjoy a good time with family.

Peach and Clotted Cream Stuffed French Toast

Prep Time: 15 minutes / Cook Time: 15 minutes / Servings: 4 / Mode: Bake

Ingredients:
- 8 slices brioche bread
- 3 large eggs
- 1 teaspoon vanilla extract
- 2 ripe peaches, thinly sliced
- 240ml whole milk
- Butter for greasing
- 100g clotted cream
- 50g sugar

Preparation Instructions:
1. Preheat the Tower Dual Basket Air Fryer to 350°F in Bake mode.
2. Spread clotted cream on 4 slices of brioche bread and top with sliced peaches.
3. Place the remaining 4 slices on top to form sandwiches.
4. In a bowl, whisk together eggs, milk, sugar, and vanilla extract.
5. Dip each sandwich into the egg mixture, ensuring it is well-coated.
6. Grease the air fryer basket with butter.
7. Place the stuffed French toast in the basket.
8. Bake for about 15 minutes until golden brown.
9. Serve warm and enjoy for a relishing breakfast experience.

Bacon-Wrapped Apricot Bites

Prep Time: 15 minutes / Cook Time: 10 minutes / Servings: 4 / Mode: Air Fry

Ingredients:
- 8 dried apricots
- 4 slices bacon, cut in half
- 30g goat cheese, crumbled
- 1 tablespoon honey
- Fresh thyme leaves for garnish

Preparation Instructions:
1. Preheat the Tower Dual Basket Air Fryer to 375°F in Air Fry mode.
2. Cut a slit in each dried apricot to create a pocket.
3. Stuff each apricot with crumbled goat cheese.
4. Wrap each apricot with half a slice of bacon, securing with a toothpick.
5. Place the bacon-wrapped apricots in the air fryer basket.
6. Air fry for about 10 minutes until the bacon is crispy.
7. Drizzle honey over the bites and garnish with fresh thyme leaves.
8. Serve warm for the best breakfast experience you've had in a while.

Cherry Tomato Tarte Tatin

Prep Time: 20 minutes / Cook Time: 25 minutes / Servings: 4 / Mode: Roast

Ingredients:
- 1 sheet puff pastry, thawed
- 2 tablespoons olive oil
- 1 tablespoon balsamic vinegar
- 1 teaspoon sugar
- Salt and pepper to taste
- 250g cherry tomatoes, halved
- 50g goat cheese, crumbled
- Fresh basil leaves for garnish

Preparation Instructions:
1. Preheat the Tower Dual Basket Air Fryer to 400°F in Roast mode.
2. Roll out the puff pastry and cut it into a circle to fit the air fryer basket.
3. In a bowl, mix olive oil, balsamic vinegar, sugar, salt, and pepper.
4. Toss cherry tomatoes in the olive oil mixture until coated.
5. Grease the air fryer basket and place the puff pastry circle in it.
6. Arrange the cherry tomatoes on the pastry, cut side down.
7. Roast for about 25 minutes until the tomatoes caramelise.
8. Carefully invert the tarte onto a plate, sprinkle with crumbled goat cheese, and garnish with fresh basil leaves.
9. Serve warm and enjoy.

caramelised Onion and Cheddar Breakfast Muffins

Prep Time: 15 minutes / Cook Time: 20 minutes / Servings: 6 / Mode: Bake

Ingredients:

- 1 tablespoon olive oil
- 250g all-purpose flour
- 2 large eggs
- 2 large onions, thinly sliced
- 1 tablespoon baking powder
- 240ml milk
- 200g cheddar cheese, grated
- 1/2 teaspoon salt
- 60ml melted butter

Preparation Instructions:

1. Preheat the Tower Dual Basket Air Fryer to 375°F in Bake mode.
2. In a pan, heat olive oil and sauté thinly sliced onions until caramelised.
3. In a large bowl, combine flour, baking powder, and salt.
4. In another bowl, whisk together eggs, milk, and melted butter.
5. Pour the wet ingredients into the dry mixture, stirring until just combined.
6. Fold in caramelised onions and grated cheddar cheese.
7. Grease the muffin cups in the air fryer basket.
8. Spoon the batter into the cups, filling each two-thirds full.
9. Bake for about 20 minutes until the tops are golden brown.
10. Allow muffins to cool slightly before serving.

Kedgeree Breakfast Bake

Prep Time: 20 minutes / Cook Time: 30 minutes / Servings: 4 / Mode: Roast

Ingredients:

- 200g cooked basmati rice
- 1 tablespoon curry powder
- 1 red bell pepper, diced
- Fresh parsley for garnish
- 200g smoked haddock, flaked
- 1 tablespoon vegetable oil
- 240ml milk
- 4 hard-boiled eggs, sliced
- 1 onion, finely chopped
- Salt and pepper to taste

Preparation Instructions:

1. Preheat the Tower Dual Basket Air Fryer to 400°F in Roast mode.
2. In a pan, heat vegetable oil and sauté chopped onion and diced bell pepper until softened.
3. Stir in curry powder and cook for an additional minute.
4. In a bowl, mix cooked basmati rice, flaked smoked haddock, sautéed vegetables, and sliced hard-boiled eggs.
5. Transfer the mixture to a greased baking dish that fits in the air fryer basket.
6. Pour milk over the mixture and season with salt and pepper.
7. Roast for about 30 minutes until the top is golden and the bake is heated through.
8. Garnish with fresh parsley before serving.

caramelised Banana Oatmeal Bars

Prep Time: 15 minutes / Cook Time: 25 minutes / Servings: 8 / Mode: Bake

Ingredients:

- 120ml melted coconut oil
- 5ml vanilla extract
- 2.5g baking soda
- 2 ripe bananas, mashed (about 240g)
- 200g rolled oats
- 50g dark chocolate chips (optional)
- 80ml maple syrup
- 60g almond flour
- 1.25g salt

Preparation Instructions:

1. Preheat the Tower Dual Basket Air Fryer to 350°F in Bake mode.
2. In a bowl, combine mashed bananas, melted coconut oil, maple syrup, and vanilla extract.
3. In another bowl, mix rolled oats, almond flour, baking soda, and salt.
4. Combine wet and dry ingredients, stirring until well incorporated.
5. Fold in dark chocolate chips if desired.

6. Grease a baking dish that fits in the air fryer basket.
7. Press the mixture into the dish evenly.
8. Bake for about 25 minutes until the edges are golden brown.
9. Allow to cool before cutting into bars.
10. Serve and enjoy!

Baked Avocado with Eggs and Chorizo

Prep Time: 10 minutes / Cook Time: 15 minutes / Servings: 2 / Mode: Roast

Ingredients:
- 2 ripe avocados
- 2 eggs
- 100g chorizo, diced
- Salt and pepper to taste
- Fresh cilantro for garnish (optional)

Preparation Instructions:
1. Preheat the Tower Dual Basket Air Fryer to 375°F in Roast mode.
2. Cut avocados in half and scoop out a bit of flesh to make room for eggs.
3. Place avocado halves in the air fryer basket.
4. Crack an egg into each avocado half.
5. Sprinkle diced chorizo over the eggs.
6. Season with salt and pepper to taste.
7. Roast for about 15 minutes until the eggs are cooked to your liking.
8. Garnish with fresh cilantro if desired.

Pesto and Sundried Tomato Breakfast Pizza

Prep Time: 15 minutes / Cook Time: 12 minutes / Servings: 2 / Mode: Bake

Ingredients:
- 1 sheet puff pastry, thawed
- 2 tablespoons pesto sauce
- 50g sundried tomatoes, sliced
- 2 large eggs
- Salt and pepper to taste
- Fresh basil leaves for garnish (optional)

Preparation Instructions:
1. Preheat the Tower Dual Basket Air Fryer to 375°F in Bake mode.
2. Roll out the puff pastry and place it in the air fryer basket.
3. Spread pesto sauce evenly over the pastry.
4. Scatter sliced sundried tomatoes on top.
5. Create two wells in the toppings for the eggs.
6. Crack an egg into each well.
7. Season with salt and pepper to taste.
8. Bake for about 12 minutes until the pastry is golden and the eggs are cooked to your liking.
9. Garnish with fresh basil leaves if desired.
10. Serve warm for a delightful breakfast treat.

Cinnamon Roll Waffles

Prep Time: 10 minutes / Cook Time: 8 minutes / Servings: 4 / Mode: Bake

Ingredients:
- 1 can refrigerated cinnamon roll dough
- Cooking spray or melted butter for greasing
- Maple syrup and icing from the cinnamon rolls for drizzling

Preparation Instructions:
1. Preheat the Tower Dual Basket Air Fryer to 350°F in Bake mode.

2. Separate the cinnamon roll dough and place each roll in the preheated air fryer basket, leaving space between them.
3. Grease the basket with cooking spray or melted butter to prevent sticking.
4. Bake for about 8 minutes until the cinnamon rolls are golden brown and cooked through.
5. Drizzle with maple syrup and icing from the cinnamon rolls.
6. Serve warm and enjoy this delightful twist on classic cinnamon rolls.

Guacamole Breakfast Bruschetta

Prep Time: 15 minutes / Cook Time: 5 minutes / Servings: 2 / Mode: Bake

Ingredients:

- 4 slices whole-grain bread
- 1 small tomato, diced
- 15ml lime juice
- Poached eggs for topping
- 1 ripe avocado, mashed (about 200g)
- 25g red onion, finely chopped
- Salt and pepper to taste
- Fresh cilantro for garnish

Preparation Instructions:

1. Preheat the Tower Dual Basket Air Fryer to 375°F in Bake mode.
2. Place whole-grain bread slices in the air fryer basket.
3. Toast the bread for about 5 minutes until crisp.
4. In a bowl, combine mashed avocado, diced tomato, red onion, lime juice, salt, and pepper.
5. Spread the guacamole mixture on the toasted bread slices.
6. Top each slice with a poached egg.
7. Garnish with fresh cilantro.
8. Serve immediately for a delicious and nutritious breakfast.

Raspberry Almond Breakfast Quinoa

Prep Time: 10 minutes / Cook Time: 15 minutes / Servings: 2 / Mode: Roast

Ingredients:

- 120g quinoa, rinsed
- 150g fresh raspberries
- Greek yoghurt for serving
- 240ml almond milk
- 15ml honey
- 30g slivered almonds, toasted
- 2.5ml almond extract

Preparation Instructions:

1. Preheat the Tower Dual Basket Air Fryer to 375°F in Roast mode.
2. In a saucepan, combine quinoa and almond milk. Bring to a boil, then reduce heat and simmer for 15 minutes or until quinoa is cooked.
3. Fluff the quinoa with a fork and stir in toasted slivered almonds, fresh raspberries, honey, and almond extract.
4. Spread the mixture in the air fryer basket.
5. Roast for about 5 minutes until the raspberries are slightly softened.
6. Serve the breakfast quinoa with a dollop of Greek yoghurt.
7. Enjoy a delightful and nutritious breakfast option.

Sweet Potato Hash with Pecans

Prep Time: 15 minutes / Cook Time: 20 minutes / Servings: 2 / Mode: Roast

Ingredients:

- 2 medium sweet potatoes, diced
- 60g pecans, chopped
- 1/2 red onion, finely chopped
- 2 tablespoons olive oil

- 1 teaspoon smoked paprika
- Fresh parsley for garnish
- Salt and pepper to taste

Preparation Instructions:
1. Preheat the Tower Dual Basket Air Fryer to 375°F in Roast mode.
2. In a bowl, toss diced sweet potatoes, chopped red onion, and pecans with olive oil and smoked paprika.
3. Spread the mixture in the air fryer basket.
4. Roast for about 20 minutes, tossing halfway through, until sweet potatoes are tender and pecans are toasted.
5. Season with salt and pepper to taste.
6. Garnish with fresh parsley.
7. Serve the sweet potato hash hot.

Pistachio and Cranberry Granola Bars

Prep Time: 15 minutes / Assembly Time: 10 minutes / Servings: 8 / Mode: Bake

Ingredients:
- 80g rolled oats (80g)
- 60ml honey
- 1/4 teaspoon salt
- 60g pistachios, chopped
- 60ml almond butter
- 40g dried cranberries, chopped
- 1 teaspoon vanilla extract

Preparation Instructions:
1. Preheat the Tower Dual Basket Air Fryer to 350°F in Bake mode.
2. In a bowl, mix rolled oats, chopped pistachios, and dried cranberries.
3. In a saucepan, warm honey and almond butter over low heat until smooth. Remove from heat and stir in vanilla extract and salt.
4. Pour the wet mixture over the dry ingredients and mix until well combined.
5. Press the mixture into a lined baking dish that fits in the air fryer basket.
6. Bake for about 15 minutes until the edges are golden.
7. Allow the granola bars to cool before cutting into squares.
8. Enjoy these tasty and nutritious granola bars as a snack or breakfast option.

Brie and Cranberry Stuffed French Toast

Prep Time: 15 minutes / Cook Time: 10 minutes / Servings: 2 / Mode: Bake

Ingredients:
- 4 slices thick-cut bread
- 2 eggs
- 1/2 teaspoon cinnamon
- 100g Brie cheese, sliced
- 120ml milk
- Butter for greasing
- 4 tablespoons cranberry sauce
- 1 teaspoon vanilla extract
- Maple syrup for serving

Preparation Instructions:
1. Preheat the Tower Dual Basket Air Fryer to 350°F in Bake mode.
2. Spread cranberry sauce on two slices of bread.
3. Layer Brie slices on top of the cranberry sauce and sandwich with the remaining bread slices.
4. In a bowl, whisk together eggs, milk, vanilla extract, and cinnamon.
5. Dip each stuffed sandwich into the egg mixture, ensuring both sides are coated.
6. Grease the air fryer basket with butter.
7. Place the stuffed sandwiches in the basket.
8. Bake for about 10 minutes until the French toast is golden brown and the Brie is melted.
9. Serve with a drizzle of maple syrup.

Fig and Prosciutto Breakfast Wraps

Prep Time: 10 minutes / Cook Time: 5 minutes / Servings: 2 / Mode: Roast

Ingredients:

- 2 large tortillas
- 4 slices prosciutto
- 4 tablespoons cream cheese
- Handful of arugula
- 4 fresh figs, sliced

Preparation Instructions:

1. Preheat the Tower Dual Basket Air Fryer to 375°F in Roast mode.
2. Spread 2 tablespoons of cream cheese on each tortilla.
3. Arrange sliced figs, prosciutto, and arugula on each tortilla.
4. Roll up the tortillas into wraps.
5. Place the wraps in the air fryer basket.
6. Roast for about 5 minutes until the wraps are heated through and slightly crispy.
7. Serve these delightful fig and prosciutto breakfast wraps warm.

Chai Spiced Porridge with Poached Pears

Prep Time: 10 minutes / Cook Time: 20 minutes / Servings: 4 / Mode: Roast

Ingredients:

- 160g steel-cut oats
- 2 tablespoons maple syrup
- 4 ripe pears, peeled and poached
- 960ml water
- 1 teaspoon chai spice blend
- Chopped nuts for garnish (optional)
- 240ml almond milk
- Pinch of salt

Preparation Instructions:

1. Preheat the Tower Dual Basket Air Fryer to 375°F in Roast mode.
2. In a saucepan, bring water to a boil, then add steel-cut oats and reduce heat. Simmer for 15-20 minutes until oats are cooked.
3. Stir in almond milk, maple syrup, chai spice blend, and a pinch of salt. Simmer for an additional 5 minutes.
4. Peel and poach the ripe pears separately.
5. Divide the chai spiced porridge among four bowls.
6. Top each serving with poached pears and sprinkle with chopped nuts if desired.
7. Serve warm, enjoying the comforting flavours of chai-spiced porridge.

Lobster Benedict

Prep Time: 20 minutes / Cook Time: 10 minutes / Servings: 4 / Mode: Bake

Ingredients:

- 4 English muffins, split and toasted
- 4 large eggs, poached
- Hollandaise sauce
- 400g lobster meat, cooked and chopped
- Fresh chives for garnish

Preparation Instructions:

1. Preheat the Tower Dual Basket Air Fryer to 350°F in Bake mode.
2. Place split and toasted English muffins on a baking tray in the air fryer basket.
3. Divide the cooked and chopped lobster meat among the English muffin halves.
4. Top each muffin with a poached egg.
5. Drizzle hollandaise sauce over the eggs.
6. Bake for about 10 minutes until the eggs are cooked to your liking.
7. Garnish with fresh chives.
8. Serve the lobster Benedict warm for a decadent breakfast or brunch.

Matcha Pancakes with Black Sesame Syrup

Prep Time: 15 minutes / Cook Time: 10 minutes / Servings: 4 / Mode: Air Fry

Ingredients:

- 120g all-purpose flour
- 1 teaspoon baking powder
- 240ml buttermilk
- Black sesame syrup for topping
- 2 tablespoons sugar
- 1/2 teaspoon baking soda
- 1 large egg
- 1 tablespoon matcha powder
- Pinch of salt
- 2 tablespoons melted butter

Preparation Instructions:

1. Preheat the Tower Dual Basket Air Fryer to 375°F in Air Fry mode.
2. In a bowl, whisk together flour, sugar, matcha powder, baking powder, baking soda, and a pinch of salt.
3. In another bowl, mix buttermilk, egg, and melted butter.
4. Pour the wet ingredients into the dry ingredients and stir until just combined.
5. Grease the air fryer basket and spoon the pancake batter into rounds.
6. Air fry for about 5 minutes per side until the pancakes are golden brown.
7. Serve with black sesame syrup for a unique and delicious twist.

caramelised Banana Oatmeal Bars

Prep Time: 15 minutes / Cook Time: 25 minutes / Servings: 8 / Mode: Bake

Ingredients:

- 80g rolled oats
- 60g almond butter
- Pinch of salt
- 2 ripe bananas, mashed
- 1 teaspoon vanilla extract
- 30g chopped walnuts
- 60ml maple syrup
- 1/2 teaspoon cinnamon

Preparation Instructions:

1. Preheat the Tower Dual Basket Air Fryer to 350°F in Bake mode.
2. In a bowl, combine rolled oats, mashed bananas, maple syrup, almond butter, vanilla extract, cinnamon, a pinch of salt, and chopped walnuts.
3. Press the mixture into a lined baking dish that fits in the air fryer basket.
4. Bake for about 25 minutes until the edges are golden.
5. Allow the oatmeal bars to cool before cutting into squares.
6. Enjoy these wholesome and flavourful caramelised banana oatmeal bars.

Crumpet Pizzas with Goat Cheese and Prosciutto

Prep Time: 10 minutes / Cook Time: 8 minutes / Servings: 4 / Mode: Air Fry

Ingredients:

- 4 crumpets
- Handful of arugula
- 120g goat cheese, crumbled
- Olive oil for drizzling
- 4 slices prosciutto
- Balsamic glaze for topping

Preparation Instructions:

1. Preheat the Tower Dual Basket Air Fryer to 375°F in Air Fry mode.
2. Place crumpets in the air fryer basket.
3. Top each crumpet with crumbled goat cheese.
4. Air fry for about 5 minutes until the crumpets are toasted and the goat cheese is slightly melted.
5. Remove crumpets from the air fryer.
6. Arrange a slice of prosciutto on each crumpet.
7. Add a handful of fresh arugula on top.
8. Drizzle with olive oil and finish with a touch of balsamic glaze.
9. Serve these delightful crumpet pizzas as a tasty breakfast option.

Lunch

Ploughman's Lunch

Prep Time: 15 minutes / Cook Time: 5 minutes / Servings: 2 / Mode: Roast

Ingredients:

- 150g cheddar cheese, cubed
- 150g ham, sliced
- 1 apple, sliced
- 1/2 cucumber, sliced
- 4 small pickles
- 4 slices of crusty bread
- Butter for spreading
- Dijon mustard for dipping

Preparation Instructions:

1. Preheat the Tower Dual Basket Air Fryer to 375°F in Roast mode.
2. Arrange cheddar cheese, ham, apple slices, cucumber slices, and pickles on a serving platter.
3. Slice the crusty bread and spread with butter.
4. Place bread slices in the air fryer basket and roast for about 5 minutes until golden and crispy.
5. Serve the roasted bread alongside the platter of cheese, ham, apple, cucumber, and pickles.
6. Add a dollop of Dijon mustard for dipping.
7. Enjoy this classic Ploughman's Lunch with family and friends for the best lunch time together.

Coronation Chicken Sandwich

Prep Time: 20 minutes / Cook Time: 5 minutes / Servings: 2 / Mode: Air Fry

Ingredients:

- 200g cooked chicken, shredded
- 2 tablespoons mayonnaise
- 1 tablespoon mango chutney
- 1 teaspoon curry powder
- 1/4 teaspoon cayenne pepper
- Salt and pepper to taste
- 4 slices whole-grain bread
- Butter for spreading
- Fresh lettuce leaves

Preparation Instructions:

1. Preheat the Tower Dual Basket Air Fryer to 375°F in Air Fry mode.
2. In a bowl, mix shredded chicken, mayonnaise, mango chutney, curry powder, cayenne pepper, salt, and pepper.
3. Spread butter on one side of each slice of whole-grain bread.
4. Place bread slices in the air fryer basket, buttered side down.
5. Air fry for about 5 minutes until the bread is toasted.
6. Spread the coronation chicken mixture on the untoasted side of two bread slices.
7. Top with fresh lettuce leaves and cover with the remaining slices.
8. Slice the sandwiches in half and serve.
9. Enjoy the rich and flavourful Coronation Chicken Sandwich for a satisfying lunch option.

Steak and Kidney Pie

Prep Time: 20 minutes / Cook Time: 1 hour 30 minutes / Servingss: 4 / Mode: Bake

Ingredients:

- 500g beef steak, cubed
- 250g beef kidney, diced
- 1 onion, chopped
- 2 carrots, diced
- 2 tablespoons all-purpose flour
- 300ml beef broth
- 150ml ale
- 2 tablespoons tomato paste
- 2 sprigs thyme
- Salt and pepper to taste
- Puff pastry sheets for topping

Preparation Instructions:

1. Preheat the Tower Dual Basket Air Fryer to 375°F in Bake mode.

2. In a large bowl, coat beef steak and kidney with flour, salt, and pepper.
3. In a pan, brown the coated meat cubes.
4. Add chopped onion and cook until softened.
5. Transfer the meat and onion to the air fryer basket.
6. Pour in beef broth, ale, tomato paste, and add diced carrots and thyme sprigs.
7. Bake for about 1 hour 30 minutes until the meat is tender and the sauce has thickened.
8. Roll out puff pastry sheets and place them on top of the pie filling.
9. Bake for an additional 15 minutes or until the pastry is golden brown.
10. Serve this classic Steak and Kidney Pie piping hot.

Steak and Ale Stew

Prep Time: 15 minutes / Cook Time: 1.5 hours / Servings: 4 / Mode: Roast

Ingredients:
- 500g beef stewing meat, cubed
- 2 carrots, sliced
- 500ml beef broth
- Salt and pepper to taste
- 1 onion, chopped
- 200g mushrooms, sliced
- 2 tablespoons tomato paste
- 2 cloves garlic, minced
- 300ml ale
- 2 bay leaves

Preparation Instructions:
1. Preheat the Tower Dual Basket Air Fryer to 375°F in Roast mode.
2. In a bowl, season beef stewing meat with salt and pepper.
3. Brown the seasoned meat in the air fryer basket.
4. Add chopped onion and minced garlic, cooking until softened.
5. Pour in ale, beef broth, and add sliced carrots, mushrooms, tomato paste, and bay leaves.
6. Roast for about 1.5 hours until the meat is tender and the stew has thickened.
7. Adjust seasoning if needed and discard bay leaves before serving.
8. Ladle this hearty Steak and Ale Stew into bowls and enjoy the comforting flavours.

Plaice with Brown Shrimp Butter

Prep Time: 10 minutes / Cook Time: 15 minutes / Servings: 2 / Mode: Roast

Ingredients:
- 2 plaice fillets
- 1 lemon, juiced
- 50g brown shrimp
- Fresh parsley, chopped
- 2 tablespoons unsalted butter
- Salt and pepper to taste

Preparation Instructions:
1. Preheat the Tower Dual Basket Air Fryer to 375°F in Roast mode.
2. Season plaice fillets with salt and pepper.
3. Place the fillets in the air fryer basket.
4. Roast for about 10-12 minutes until the fish is cooked through and flakes easily.
5. In a small pan, melt unsalted butter.
6. Add brown shrimp to the melted butter and cook until they turn pink.
7. Stir in lemon juice and chopped fresh parsley.
8. Pour the brown shrimp butter sauce over the roasted plaice fillets.
9. Garnish with additional fresh parsley.
10. Serve this Plaice with Brown Shrimp Butter alongside your favorite side dishes for a delightful seafood meal.

Lancashire Cheese and Onion Pie

Prep Time: 20 minutes / Cook Time: 45 minutes / Servings: 4 / Mode: Bake

Ingredients:
- 300g Lancashire cheese, grated
- 200ml whole milk
- Shortcrust pastry sheets
- 2 large onions, finely sliced
- 2 tablespoons all-purpose flour
- 2 tablespoons butter
- Salt and pepper to taste

Preparation Instructions:
1. Preheat the Tower Dual Basket Air Fryer to 375°F in Bake mode.
2. In a pan, sauté finely sliced onions in butter until softened.
3. Stir in all-purpose flour, then slowly add whole milk, continuously stirring until smooth.
4. Add grated Lancashire cheese and season with salt and pepper.
5. Roll out shortcrust pastry sheets and line the air fryer basket.
6. Pour the cheese and onion mixture onto the pastry.
7. Top with another layer of pastry, sealing the edges.
8. Bake for about 45 minutes until the pastry is golden and the filling is cooked.
9. Allow the Lancashire Cheese and Onion Pie to cool slightly before slicing and serving.

Quiche Lorraine

Prep Time: 20 minutes / Cook Time: 40 minutes / Servings: 6 / Mode: Bake

Ingredients:
- 1 pre-made pie crust
- 4 large eggs
- 200g bacon, cooked and crumbled
- Salt and pepper to taste
- 240ml heavy cream
- Nutmeg for seasoning

Preparation Instructions:
1. Preheat the Tower Dual Basket Air Fryer to 375°F in Bake mode.
2. Roll out the pre-made pie crust and line the air fryer basket.
3. In a bowl, whisk together 240ml of heavy cream, 4 large eggs, salt, pepper, and a pinch of nutmeg.
4. Sprinkle cooked and crumbled bacon evenly over the pie crust.
5. Pour the egg and cream mixture over the bacon.
6. Sprinkle shredded Gruyère cheese on top.
7. Bake for about 40 minutes until the quiche is set and the crust is golden.
8. Allow the Quiche Lorraine to cool for a few minutes before slicing.
9. Serve warm and enjoy this classic French quiche!

Chicken and Vegetable Pasty

Prep Time: 20 minutes / Cook Time: 25 minutes / Servings: 4 / Mode: Air Fry

Ingredients:
- 300g cooked chicken, shredded
- 200g mixed vegetables (carrots, peas, corn), diced
- 1 teaspoon dried thyme
- 1 egg, beaten (for egg wash)
- 1 onion, finely chopped
- 2 tablespoons olive oil
- Salt and pepper to taste
- 2 sheets ready-made puff pastry

Preparation Instructions:
1. Preheat the Tower Dual Basket Air Fryer to 375°F in Air Fry mode.
2. In a pan, sauté finely chopped onion in olive oil until softened.
3. Add diced mixed vegetables and cook until slightly tender.
4. Stir in shredded cooked chicken, dried thyme, salt, and pepper. Cook for an additional 2 minutes.
5. Roll out the ready-made puff pastry sheets and cut into squares.
6. Spoon the chicken and vegetable mixture onto one half of each pastry square.
7. Fold the pastry over the filling, creating a triangle, and press the edges to seal.
8. Brush each pasty with beaten egg for a golden finish.

9. Place the pasties in the air fryer basket without touching each other.

10. Air fry for about 25 minutes or until the pasties are golden and crisp.

11. Allow the Chicken and Vegetable Pasties to cool slightly before serving.

12. Enjoy a delicious and convenient lunch with this hearty and flavourful recipe!

Plaice with Lemon and Parsley Butter

Prep Time: 10 minutes / Cook Time: 15 minutes / Servings: 2 / Mode: Roast

Ingredients:
- 2 plaice fillets
- 1 lemon, zest and juice
- Salt and pepper to taste
- 2 tablespoons unsalted butter, melted
- 2 tablespoons fresh parsley, chopped

Preparation Instructions:
1. Preheat the Tower Dual Basket Air Fryer to 375°F in Roast mode.
2. Season plaice fillets with salt and pepper.
3. In a small bowl, mix melted unsalted butter, lemon zest, lemon juice, and chopped fresh parsley.
4. Place the plaice fillets in the air fryer basket.
5. Drizzle the lemon and parsley butter mixture over the fillets.
6. Roast for about 10-12 minutes until the fish is cooked through and flakes easily.
7. Baste the plaice fillets with the butter mixture during cooking for extra flavour.
8. Garnish with additional fresh parsley before serving.
9. Serve this Plaice with Lemon and Parsley Butter with your favorite side dishes.

Mushroom and Spinach Risotto

Prep Time: 15 minutes / Cook Time: 25 minutes / Servings: 4 / Mode: Bake

Ingredients:
- 300g Arborio rice
- 1 onion, finely chopped
- 150ml dry white wine
- Salt and pepper to taste
- 200g mushrooms, sliced
- 2 cloves garlic, minced
- 50g Parmesan cheese, grated
- 150g fresh spinach
- 1 liter vegetable broth, heated
- 2 tablespoons olive oil

Preparation Instructions:
1. Preheat the Tower Dual Basket Air Fryer to 375°F in Bake mode.
2. In a pan, sauté finely chopped onion and minced garlic in olive oil until softened.
3. Add Arborio rice and cook until lightly toasted.
4. Pour in dry white wine and cook until the wine is mostly absorbed.
5. Add sliced mushrooms and cook until they release their moisture.
6. Gradually add heated vegetable broth, one ladle at a time, stirring constantly.
7. Continue this process until the rice is creamy and cooked to al dente.
8. Stir in fresh spinach and grated Parmesan cheese.
9. Season with salt and pepper to taste.
10. Bake in the air fryer for an additional 5 minutes until the risotto is heated through.
11. Serve this Mushroom and Spinach Risotto as a comforting and flavourful main dish.
12. Enjoy the rich and creamy texture of this delightful risotto!

Fisherman's Pie

Prep Time: 20 minutes / Cook Time: 30 minutes / Servings: 4 / Mode: Bake

Ingredients:
- 400g white fish fillets, cubed
- 200g cooked and peeled prawns
- 1 onion, finely chopped

- 2 carrots, diced
- 300ml whole milk
- 800g mashed potatoes
- Fresh parsley, chopped (for garnish)
- 200g frozen peas
- 2 tablespoons all-purpose flour
- Salt and pepper to taste
- 300ml fish stock
- 2 tablespoons butter

Preparation Instructions:
1. Preheat the Tower Dual Basket Air Fryer to 375°F in Bake mode.
2. In a pan, melt butter and sauté finely chopped onion until softened.
3. Stir in all-purpose flour to create a roux.
4. Gradually add fish stock and whole milk, stirring constantly until smooth.
5. Add diced carrots and cook until slightly tender.
6. Add cubed white fish fillets and cooked prawns, cooking until the fish is opaque.
7. Stir in frozen peas and season with salt and pepper to taste.
8. Transfer the fish mixture to a baking dish.
9. Spoon mashed potatoes over the fish mixture, creating an even layer.
10. Bake for about 30 minutes until the top is golden and the filling is bubbling.
11. Garnish with chopped fresh parsley before serving.
12. Enjoy this comforting and hearty Fisherman's Pie, a classic British dish!

Chicken Tikka Wraps

Prep Time: 15 minutes / Cook Time: 20 minutes / Servings: 4 / Mode: Air Fry

Ingredients:
- 500g boneless, skinless chicken thighs, cut into bite-sized pieces
- 4 tablespoons Greek yoghurt
- 1 teaspoon ground coriander
- 4 whole-grain wraps
- 4 tablespoons mint yoghurt sauce
- 2 tablespoons tikka masala paste
- 1 teaspoon paprika
- Fresh salad greens (lettuce, tomatoes, cucumbers)
- 1 teaspoon ground cumin
- Salt and pepper to taste

Preparation Instructions:
1. In a bowl, mix Greek yoghurt, tikka masala paste, ground cumin, ground coriander, paprika, salt, and pepper.
2. Add chicken pieces to the marinade, ensuring they are well-coated. Marinate for at least 15 minutes.
3. Preheat the Tower Dual Basket Air Fryer to 375°F in Air Fry mode.
4. Place marinated chicken pieces in the air fryer basket, making sure they are not overcrowded.
5. Air fry for about 15-20 minutes until the chicken is cooked through and has a nice char.
6. While the chicken is cooking, warm the whole-grain wraps.
7. Assemble the wraps with fresh salad greens and the air-fried chicken.
8. Drizzle each wrap with mint yoghurt sauce.
9. Roll up the wraps, securing them with toothpicks if needed.
10. Serve hot and enjoy with family and friends!

Turkey and Cranberry Panini

Prep Time: 15 minutes / Cook Time: 10 minutes / Servings: 2 / Mode: Air Fry or Panini Press

Ingredients:
- 200g sliced turkey breast
- 100g Brie cheese, sliced
- 100g cranberry sauce
- Butter for spreading
- 4 slices whole-grain bread

Preparation Instructions:
1. Preheat the Tower Dual Basket Air Fryer to 375°F in Air Fry mode or use a Panini press.
2. Lay out the slices of whole-grain bread.

3. Spread butter on one side of each bread slice.

4. On the unbuttered side of two slices, layer sliced turkey, cranberry sauce, and Brie cheese.

5. Place the remaining bread slices on top to create sandwiches.

6. If using the Air Fryer, place the sandwiches in the air fryer basket without touching each other.

7. Air fry for about 8-10 minutes until the bread is golden and the filling is heated through.

8. If using a Panini press, follow the manufacturer's instructions.

9. Allow the Turkey and Cranberry Panini to cool slightly before serving.

10. Enjoy this festive and flavourful panini!

Grilled Portobello Mushroom Salad

Prep Time: 15 minutes / Cook Time: 15 minutes / Servings: 2 / Mode: Grill or Roast

Ingredients:

- 2 large Portobello mushrooms, cleaned and sliced
- 2 cloves garlic, minced
- Mixed salad greens (lettuce, spinach, arugula)
- Balsamic vinaigrette dressing
- 2 tablespoons olive oil
- Fresh thyme leaves
- 150g cherry tomatoes, halved

Preparation Instructions:

1. Preheat the Tower Dual Basket Air Fryer to 375°F in Roast mode or use a grill.

2. In a bowl, combine sliced Portobello mushrooms, olive oil, minced garlic, and fresh thyme leaves.

3. If using the Air Fryer, place the marinated mushrooms in the air fryer basket.

4. Roast for about 15 minutes until the mushrooms are tender and slightly charred.

5. If using a grill, cook the mushrooms until they are tender.

6. In a large bowl, combine mixed salad greens and cherry tomatoes.

7. Add the grilled Portobello mushrooms to the salad.

8. Drizzle with balsamic vinaigrette dressing and toss to combine.

9. Serve this Grilled Portobello Mushroom Salad as a hearty and flavourful alternative.

10. Enjoy a satisfying and nutritious salad!

Grilled Chicken Caesar Salad

Prep Time: 20 minutes / Cook Time: 15 minutes / Servings: 2 / Mode: Roast

Ingredients:

- 2 boneless, skinless chicken breasts
- Romaine lettuce, chopped
- Caesar dressing
- 1 tablespoon olive oil
- 60g croutons
- Salt and pepper to taste
- 50g Parmesan cheese, shaved

Preparation Instructions:

1. Preheat the Tower Dual Basket Air Fryer to 375°F in Roast mode or use a grill.

2. Rub chicken breasts with olive oil and season with salt and pepper.

3. If using the Air Fryer, place the chicken breasts in the air fryer basket.

4. Roast for about 15 minutes until the chicken is cooked through.

5. If using a grill, cook the chicken until it reaches an internal temperature of 165°F.

6. Slice the grilled chicken into strips.

7. In a large bowl, toss chopped Romaine lettuce with croutons, shaved Parmesan cheese, and grilled chicken strips.

8. Drizzle Caesar dressing over the salad and toss to combine.

9. Serve this Grilled Chicken Caesar Salad as a satisfying and flavourful lunch meal.

Smoked Salmon Bagel

Prep Time: 10 minutes / Cook Time: 5 minutes / Servings: 2 / Mode: Air Fry

Ingredients:

- 2 whole-grain bagels, sliced
- Red onion, thinly sliced
- Lemon wedges
- 100g smoked salmon
- Capers for garnish
- 4 tablespoons cream cheese
- Fresh dill for garnish

Preparation Instructions:

1. Preheat the air fryer to 350°F.
2. Place the bagel halves in the air fryer basket without overlapping.
3. Air fry for 3-5 minutes until the bagels are toasted.
4. Spread a generous layer of cream cheese on each air-fried bagel half.
5. Arrange smoked salmon on top of the cream cheese.
6. Add thinly sliced red onion and capers.
7. Garnish with fresh dill.
8. Serve the Smoked Salmon Bagel with lemon wedges on the side.
9. Enjoy this classic and delicious air-fried bagel combination!

Ham and Pease Pudding Stottie

Prep Time: 15 minutes / Cook Time: 4 minutes / Servings: 2 / Mode: Air Fry

Ingredients:

- 2 stottie bread rounds
- Mustard for spreading
- 200g cooked ham, sliced
- Mixed salad greens (optional)
- 4 tablespoons pease pudding

Preparation Instructions:

1. Preheat the air fryer to 350°F.
2. Cut the stottie bread rounds in half.
3. Place the stottie halves in the air fryer basket.
4. Air fry for 3-4 minutes until the stottie halves are warmed and slightly crispy.
5. Spread a layer of pease pudding on one half of each air-fried stottie.
6. Layer sliced cooked ham on top of the pease pudding.
7. Optionally, add a layer of mixed salad greens.
8. Spread mustard on the other half of each stottie.
9. Press the halves together gently.
10. Serve the Air Fryer Ham and Pease Pudding Stottie as a hearty and satisfying air-fried sandwich.
11. Enjoy this traditional North East England delicacy prepared in the air fryer!

Bacon and Mushroom Quiche

Prep Time: 20 minutes / Cook Time: 30 minutes / Servings: 4 / Mode: Bake

Ingredients:

- 1 pre-made pie crust (or homemade)
- 200g mushrooms, sliced
- 240ml milk
- 200g bacon, cooked and crumbled
- 100g shredded Gruyere cheese
- Salt and pepper to taste
- 4 large eggs
- Fresh chives for garnish

Preparation Instructions:

1. Preheat the Air Fryer to 375°F in Bake mode.
2. Roll out the pie crust and press it into a pie dish.
3. Cook bacon until crispy, then crumble it.

4. In a pan, sauté sliced mushrooms until they release their moisture.
5. Layer bacon, mushrooms, and shredded Gruyere cheese in the pie crust.
6. In a bowl, whisk together eggs, milk, salt, and pepper.
7. Pour the egg mixture over the bacon, mushrooms, and cheese.
8. Bake for 30 minutes or until the quiche is set and golden.
9. Garnish with fresh chives.
10. Allow the quiche to cool slightly before slicing and serving.

Duck Confit Pie

Prep Time: 30 minutes / Cook Time: 1 hour / Servings: 6 / Mode: Bake

Ingredients:
- 2 duck confit legs, shredded
- 1 onion, finely chopped
- 2 cloves garlic, minced
- 200g baby potatoes, boiled and sliced
- 160g peas
- 240ml chicken or duck stock
- 2 tablespoons all-purpose flour
- 1 pre-made pie crust (or homemade)
- Salt and pepper to taste
- Egg wash for brushing

Preparation Instructions:
1. Preheat the Air Fryer to 375°F in Bake mode.
2. In a pan, sauté chopped onion and minced garlic until softened.
3. Add shredded duck confit, boiled sliced baby potatoes, and peas to the pan.
4. Sprinkle flour over the mixture and stir to combine.
5. Gradually pour in the stock, stirring continuously until it thickens.
6. Roll out the pie crust and press it into a pie dish.
7. Pour the duck mixture into the pie crust.
8. Cover with another layer of pie crust, crimping the edges to seal.
9. Brush the top crust with egg wash for a golden finish.
10. Bake for 1 hour or until the crust is golden and the filling is bubbling.
11. Allow the Duck Confit Pie to cool slightly before serving.

Black Pudding and Apple Salad

Prep Time: 15 minutes / Cook Time: 10 minutes / Servings: 4 / Mode: Not applicable

Ingredients:
- 200g black pudding, sliced
- 2 apples, cored and thinly sliced
- 100g mixed salad greens
- 50g walnuts, toasted
- 50g feta cheese, crumbled
- 2 tablespoons olive oil
- 1 tablespoon balsamic vinegar
- Salt and pepper to taste

Preparation Instructions:
1. In a pan, cook the sliced black pudding until crispy on both sides. Set aside.
2. In a large bowl, combine mixed salad greens, thinly sliced apples, toasted walnuts, and crumbled feta cheese.
3. Drizzle olive oil and balsamic vinegar over the salad. Toss gently to coat.
4. Season the salad with salt and pepper to taste.
5. Top the salad with crispy black pudding slices.
6. Serve the Black Pudding and Apple Salad immediately.
7. Enjoy this flavourful and hearty salad as a delicious meal or side dish.

Dinner

Quorn Sausage Casserole

Prep Time: 20 minutes / Cook Time: 30 minutes / Servings: 4 / Mode: Bake

Ingredients:
- 8 Quorn sausages
- 400g can chopped tomatoes
- 1 teaspoon dried thyme
- 2 tablespoons olive oil
- 1 onion, finely chopped
- 200ml vegetable broth
- 1 teaspoon dried rosemary
- 2 garlic cloves, minced
- 1 tablespoon tomato paste
- Salt and pepper to taste

Preparation Instructions:
1. Preheat the Air Fryer to 375°F in Bake mode.
2. In a large Air Fryer-safe casserole dish, heat olive oil over medium heat.
3. Add chopped onion and garlic, sauté until softened.
4. Add Quorn sausages and brown them on all sides.
5. Pour in chopped tomatoes, vegetable broth, tomato paste, thyme, rosemary, salt, and pepper. Stir well.
6. Cover the casserole dish and transfer it to the preheated Air Fryer.
7. Bake for 30 minutes or until the sausages are cooked through.
8. Serve this hearty Quorn Sausage Casserole with your favourite side.

Pesto Crusted Rack of Lamb

Prep Time: 15 minutes / Cook Time: 25 minutes / Servings: 4 / Mode: Roast

Ingredients:
- 2 racks of lamb
- 4 tablespoons pesto sauce
- Salt and pepper to taste

Preparation Instructions:
1. Preheat the Air Fryer to 400°F in Roast mode.
2. Season the racks of lamb with salt and pepper.
3. Place the racks in a roasting pan, fat side up.
4. Spread pesto sauce evenly over the top of each rack.
5. Roast in the preheated Air Fryer for 25 minutes or until the internal temperature reaches your desired doneness.
6. Let the lamb rest for a few minutes before slicing.
7. Serve this elegant Pesto Crusted Rack of Lamb at dinner for a wonderful family time.

Mediterranean Veggie Pita Pockets

Prep Time: 15 minutes / Cook Time: 10 minutes / Servings: 4 / Mode: Air Fry

Ingredients:
- 4 whole wheat pita pockets
- 1/2 red onion, thinly sliced
- 30ml olive oil
- Salt and pepper to taste
- 150g cherry tomatoes, halved
- 100g feta cheese, crumbled
- 15ml balsamic vinegar
- Fresh parsley for garnish
- 1 cucumber, diced
- 25g Kalamata olives, sliced
- 1 teaspoon dried oregano

Preparation Instructions:
1. Preheat the air fryer to 375°F in Air Fry mode.

2. In a bowl, combine cherry tomatoes, cucumber, red onion, feta cheese, and Kalamata olives.
3. Drizzle olive oil and balsamic vinegar over the veggie mixture. Season with dried oregano, salt, and pepper. Toss gently to coat.
4. Place the whole wheat pita pockets in the air fryer basket and air fry for 3-5 minutes until warmed.
5. Stuff the warm pita pockets with the Mediterranean veggie mixture.
6. Garnish with fresh parsley before serving.

Haggis Neeps and Tatties

Prep Time: 30 minutes / Cook Time: 45 minutes / Servings: 4 / Mode: Bake

Ingredients:
- 400g haggis
- 4 large tatties (potatoes), peeled and diced
- Salt and pepper to taste
- 4 large neeps (turnips), peeled and diced
- 2 tablespoons butter

Preparation Instructions:
1. Preheat the Air Fryer to 375°F in Bake mode.
2. Cook the haggis according to package instructions.
3. Boil diced neeps and tatties until tender. Drain and mash with butter.
4. Layer the mashed neeps and tatties in a baking dish.
5. Crumble cooked haggis over the mashed vegetables.
6. Bake in the preheated Air Fryer for 30-45 minutes until the top is golden and crispy.
7. Serve this traditional Haggis Neeps and Tatties dish as a comforting meal.

Duck Confit with Orange Glaze

Prep Time: 15 minutes / Cook Time: 30 minutes / Servings: 4 / Mode: Roast

Ingredients:
- 4 duck confit legs
- 1 tablespoon soy sauce
- Salt and pepper to taste
- Zest and juice of 2 oranges
- 2 cloves garlic, minced
- Orange slices for garnish
- 2 tablespoons honey
- 1 teaspoon fresh thyme leaves

Preparation Instructions:
1. Preheat the air fryer to 375°F in Roast mode.
2. In a small bowl, mix orange zest, orange juice, honey, soy sauce, minced garlic, fresh thyme leaves, salt, and pepper to create the glaze.
3. Pat the duck confit legs dry and brush them generously with the orange glaze.
4. Place the duck legs in the air fryer basket.
5. Roast for 30 minutes, basting with the remaining glaze halfway through, until the duck skin is crispy and golden.
6. Garnish with orange slices before serving.

Lancashire Cheese and Onion Pie

Prep Time: 20 minutes / Cook Time: 30 minutes / Servings: 6 / Mode: Bake

Ingredients:
- 1 sheet shortcrust pastry (store-bought or homemade)
- 200g Lancashire cheese, grated
- Salt and pepper to taste
- 2 large onions, thinly sliced
- 2 tablespoons butter
- 1 egg, beaten (for egg wash)
- 1 tablespoon olive oil

Preparation Instructions:
1. Preheat the air fryer to 375°F in Bake mode.

2. In a pan, sauté the thinly sliced onions in butter and olive oil until caramelised. Season with salt and pepper.
3. Roll out the shortcrust pastry and line a pie dish.
4. Fill the pastry with the caramelised onions and grated Lancashire cheese.
5. Cover the filling with another layer of pastry, sealing the edges. Cut a few slits on top for ventilation.
6. Brush the pie with beaten egg for a golden finish.
7. Bake for 30 minutes or until the pastry is golden brown.
8. Allow the Lancashire Cheese and Onion Pie to cool slightly before slicing and serving.

Chicken and Bacon Carbonara

Prep Time: 15 minutes / Cook Time: 20 minutes / Servings: 4 / Mode: Air Fry

Ingredients:
- 400g spaghetti
- 3 large eggs
- Salt and black pepper to taste
- 200g chicken breast, diced
- 100g Parmesan cheese, grated
- 150g bacon, chopped
- 2 cloves garlic, minced
- Fresh parsley, chopped (for garnish)

Preparation Instructions:
1. Cook the spaghetti according to package instructions. Drain and set aside.
2. In a pan, air fry the diced chicken and chopped bacon until cooked and crispy. Set aside.
3. In a bowl, whisk together the eggs, grated Parmesan cheese, minced garlic, salt, and black pepper.
4. Toss the cooked spaghetti in the egg and cheese mixture until well coated.
5. Add the air-fried chicken and bacon to the pasta, mixing thoroughly.
6. Preheat the air fryer to 375°F in Air Fry mode.
7. Transfer the carbonara mixture to an air fryer-safe dish.
8. Air fry for 10 minutes, stirring halfway through, until the top is golden and the carbonara is heated through.
9. Garnish with chopped fresh parsley before serving.

Black Pudding and Apple Stack

Prep Time: 15 minutes / Cook Time: 10 minutes / Servings: 4 / Mode: Roast

Ingredients:
- 200g black pudding, sliced
- 30ml honey
- 2 apples, cored and sliced
- Fresh thyme leaves (for garnish)
- 50g goat cheese, crumbled

Preparation Instructions:
1. Preheat the air fryer to 375°F in Roast mode.
2. In a pan, roast the sliced black pudding until crispy on both sides. Set aside.
3. Arrange the cored and sliced apples in the air fryer basket.
4. Roast the apples for 5-7 minutes until they are tender but still hold their shape.
5. Assemble the stack by layering black pudding slices, roasted apple slices, and crumbled goat cheese.
6. Drizzle honey over the stack.
7. Roast the assembled stacks in the air fryer for an additional 3-5 minutes to melt the goat cheese.
8. Garnish with fresh thyme leaves before serving.

Venison Sausages with Red Wine Gravy

Prep Time: 15 minutes / Cook Time: 25 minutes / Servings: 4 / Mode: Roast

Ingredients:
- 8 venison sausages
- 2 cloves garlic, minced
- 2 tablespoons olive oil
- 200ml red wine
- 1 onion, finely chopped
- 300ml beef stock

- 2 tablespoons flour
- Salt and black pepper to taste
- Fresh parsley, chopped (for garnish)

Preparation Instructions:
1. Preheat the air fryer to 375°F in Roast mode.
2. In a pan, roast the venison sausages until browned on all sides. Set aside.
3. In the same pan, heat olive oil and sauté the finely chopped onion and minced garlic until softened.
4. Sprinkle flour over the onion and garlic, stirring to create a roux.
5. Gradually add red wine and beef stock to the pan, stirring continuously to avoid lumps.
6. Bring the mixture to a simmer, allowing it to thicken into a rich gravy. Season with salt and black pepper to taste.
7. Add the roasted venison sausages to the gravy, ensuring they are fully coated.
8. Transfer the sausages and gravy to an air fryer-safe dish and roast for an additional 10-15 minutes until the sausages are cooked through.
9. Garnish with chopped fresh parsley before serving.

Lamb Shank with Rosemary

Prep Time: 15 minutes / Cook Time: 2 hours / Servings: 4 / Mode: Bake

Ingredients:
- 4 lamb shanks
- 2 tablespoons olive oil
- 2 onions, chopped
- 3 carrots, peeled and chopped
- 4 cloves garlic, minced
- 750ml red wine
- 500ml beef stock
- 2 sprigs rosemary
- Salt and black pepper to taste

Preparation Instructions:
1. Preheat the air fryer to 375°F in Bake mode.
2. In a pan, sear the lamb shanks in olive oil until browned on all sides. Set aside.
3. In the same pan, sauté the chopped onions, chopped carrots, and minced garlic until softened.
4. Add red wine, beef stock, and rosemary to the pan. Bring the mixture to a simmer.
5. Season the lamb shanks with salt and black pepper, then add them back to the pan.
6. Transfer the entire mixture to an air fryer-safe dish and bake for 2 to 2.5 hours, until the lamb is tender and falls off the bone.
7. Serve the Lamb Shank with Rosemary with your choice of sides.

Chicken Marsala

Prep Time: 15 minutes / Cook Time: 25 minutes / Servings: 4 / Mode: Roast

Ingredients:
- 4 boneless, skinless chicken breasts
- Salt and black pepper to taste
- 125g all-purpose flour
- 4 tablespoons olive oil
- 8 ounces mushrooms, sliced
- 2 cloves garlic, minced
- 240ml Marsala wine
- 240ml chicken broth
- 2 tablespoons unsalted butter
- Fresh parsley, chopped (for garnish)

Preparation Instructions:
1. Preheat the air fryer to 375°F in Roast mode.
2. Season the chicken breasts with salt and black pepper, then dredge them in flour, shaking off any excess.
3. In a large pan, heat olive oil over medium-high heat. Add the chicken breasts and cook until golden brown on both sides. Transfer the chicken to the air fryer basket.
4. In the same pan, sauté the sliced mushrooms and minced garlic until the mushrooms are tender.
5. Pour in Marsala wine and chicken broth, scraping the bottom of the pan to release any browned bits. Simmer until the liquid is reduced by half.

6. Return the cooked chicken to the pan, allowing it to absorb the flavours. Add butter to create a rich sauce.
7. Transfer the chicken Marsala to the air fryer and roast for an additional 10 minutes, ensuring the chicken is cooked through.
8. Garnish with chopped fresh parsley before serving.

Grilled Tandoori Chicken

Prep Time: 20 minutes / Cook Time: 20 minutes / Servings: 4 / Mode: Air Fry

Ingredients:

- 4 boneless, skinless chicken thighs
- 2 tablespoons Tandoori spice blend
- 2 teaspoons ginger paste
- 1 teaspoon ground cumin
- Salt and black pepper to taste
- Lemon wedges (for serving)
- 240ml plain Greek yoghurt
- 1 tablespoon olive oil
- 2 teaspoons garlic paste
- 1 teaspoon ground coriander
- Fresh cilantro, chopped (for garnish)

Preparation Instructions:

1. Preheat the air fryer to 375°F in Air Fry mode.
2. In a bowl, mix together Greek yoghurt, Tandoori spice blend, olive oil, ginger paste, garlic paste, ground cumin, ground coriander, salt, and black pepper.
3. Marinate the chicken thighs in the Tandoori mixture, ensuring they are well-coated. Let them marinate for at least 15 minutes.
4. Place the marinated chicken thighs in the air fryer basket, ensuring they are not touching.
5. Air fry for 15-20 minutes until the chicken is cooked through and has a charred exterior.
6. Garnish with chopped fresh cilantro and serve with lemon wedges.

Butternut Squash Risotto

Prep Time: 15 minutes / Cook Time: 25 minutes / Servings: 4 / Mode: Bake

Ingredients:

- 300g butternut squash, diced
- 300g Arborio rice
- 50g Parmesan cheese, grated
- Fresh sage leaves (for garnish)
- 2 tablespoons olive oil
- 120ml white wine
- Salt and black pepper to taste
- 1 onion, finely chopped
- 1.5 litres vegetable broth, warmed

Preparation Instructions:

1. Preheat the air fryer to 375°F in Bake mode.
2. Toss the diced butternut squash in olive oil, season with salt and pepper, and spread it evenly in the air fryer basket. Bake for 15-20 minutes until tender.
3. In a large pan, sauté the chopped onion in olive oil until translucent. Add Arborio rice and cook until lightly toasted.
4. Pour in the white wine, stirring constantly until absorbed. Begin adding the warm vegetable broth one ladle at a time, allowing each addition to be absorbed before adding more.
5. Once the rice is creamy and al dente, fold in the roasted butternut squash and grated Parmesan. Adjust seasoning to taste.
6. Garnish with fresh sage leaves before serving.

Shrimp Scampi

Prep Time: 10 minutes / Cook Time: 15 minutes / Servings: 4 / Mode: Air Fry

Ingredients:

- 400g large shrimp, peeled and deveined
- 4 cloves garlic, minced
- Juice of 1 lemon
- Salt and red pepper flakes to taste
- 3 tablespoons olive oil
- 120ml white wine
- 2 tablespoons fresh parsley, chopped
- 300g linguine, cooked (for serving)

Preparation Instructions:

1. Preheat the air fryer to 375°F in Air Fry mode.
2. In a bowl, toss the shrimp with olive oil, minced garlic, salt, and red pepper flakes.
3. Place the shrimp in the air fryer basket and air fry for 8-10 minutes, shaking the basket halfway through.
4. In a separate pan, heat white wine and lemon juice. Add the cooked shrimp to the pan, stirring to coat them in the flavourful sauce.
5. Serve the shrimp scampi over a bed of cooked linguine, garnished with fresh parsley.

Sweet Potato and Chickpea Tagine

Prep Time: 15 minutes / Cook Time: 30 minutes / Servings: 4 / Mode: Roast

Ingredients:

- 2 sweet potatoes, peeled and diced
- 1 onion, finely chopped
- 1 teaspoon ground coriander
- 300ml vegetable broth
- Salt and pepper to taste
- 2 cloves garlic, minced
- 1 teaspoon smoked paprika
- 50g dried apricots, chopped
- Fresh cilantro (for garnish)
- 400g canned chickpeas, drained and rinsed
- 1 teaspoon ground cumin
- 400g canned diced tomatoes
- 2 tablespoons olive oil

Preparation Instructions:

1. Preheat the air fryer to 400°F in Roast mode.
2. In a large bowl, toss the diced sweet potatoes, chickpeas, chopped onion, minced garlic, ground cumin, ground coriander, smoked paprika, olive oil, salt, and pepper until evenly coated.
3. Spread the mixture in the air fryer basket and roast for 25-30 minutes, stirring halfway through, until sweet potatoes are tender and chickpeas are crispy.
4. In a saucepan, combine diced tomatoes, vegetable broth, and chopped dried apricots. Simmer over medium heat until heated through.
5. Serve the roasted sweet potato and chickpea mixture over the tomato-apricot sauce. Garnish with fresh cilantro.
6. Enjoy this flavourful Sweet Potato and Chickpea Tagine with family and friends.

Creamy Garlic Mushroom Chicken

Prep Time: 10 minutes / Cook Time: 25 minutes / Servings: 4 / Mode: Bake

Ingredients:

- 4 boneless, skinless chicken breasts
- 4 cloves garlic, minced
- 50g Parmesan cheese, grated
- 2 tablespoons olive oil
- Fresh parsley (for garnish)
- 200g mushrooms, sliced
- 200ml heavy cream
- 2 tablespoons butter
- Salt and black pepper to taste

Preparation Instructions:

1. Preheat the air fryer to 375°F in Bake mode.
2. Season chicken breasts with salt and black pepper. In a pan, heat olive oil and sear the chicken until browned on both sides. Transfer to the air fryer basket.

3. In the same pan, melt butter and sauté sliced mushrooms until tender. Add minced garlic and cook until fragrant.
4. Pour in heavy cream, stirring to combine. Add grated Parmesan and continue stirring until the sauce thickens.
5. Pour the creamy garlic mushroom sauce over the chicken in the air fryer basket.
6. Bake for 20-25 minutes until the chicken is cooked through.
7. Garnish with fresh parsley before serving. Enjoy this Creamy Garlic Mushroom Chicken.

BBQ Pulled Jackfruit Sandwiches

Prep Time: 15 minutes / Cook Time: 30 minutes / Servings: 4 / Mode: Air Fry

Ingredients:

- 2 cans (400g each) young green jackfruit, drained and shredded
- 1 onion, finely chopped
- 2 cloves garlic, minced
- 240ml barbecue sauce
- 60ml vegetable broth
- 1 tablespoon olive oil
- 1 tablespoon apple cider vinegar
- 1 teaspoon smoked paprika
- 1 teaspoon ground cumin
- 1/2 teaspoon Chilli powder
- Salt and pepper to taste
- 4 whole grain burger buns
- Coleslaw (optional, for serving)

Preparation Instructions:

1. Preheat the air fryer to 375°F in Air Fry mode.
2. In a pan, heat olive oil and sauté chopped onion until translucent. Add minced garlic and cook until fragrant.
3. Add shredded jackfruit to the pan, along with smoked paprika, ground cumin, Chilli powder, salt, and pepper. Stir to combine.
4. Pour in barbecue sauce, vegetable broth, and apple cider vinegar. Simmer over medium heat until the jackfruit absorbs the flavours and becomes tender.
5. Spread the seasoned jackfruit in the air fryer basket and air fry for 20-25 minutes, stirring occasionally, until the edges are crispy.
6. Serve the BBQ Pulled Jackfruit on whole grain burger buns. Top with coleslaw if desired.

Lentil Shepherd's Pie

Prep Time: 20 minutes / Cook Time: 30 minutes / Servings: 4 / Mode: Bake

Ingredients:

- 200g dried green lentils, rinsed and drained
- 480ml vegetable broth
- 2 tablespoons olive oil
- 1 onion, finely chopped
- 2 carrots, diced
- 2 celery stalks, diced
- 3 cloves garlic, minced
- 400g canned diced tomatoes
- 1 teaspoon dried thyme
- 1 teaspoon dried rosemary
- Salt and pepper to taste
- 800g potatoes, peeled and diced
- 60ml unsweetened almond milk
- 2 tablespoons vegan butter

Preparation Instructions:

1. Preheat the air fryer to 375°F in Bake mode.
2. In a saucepan, combine lentils and vegetable broth. Simmer until lentils are tender and most of the liquid is absorbed.
3. In a large pan, heat olive oil and sauté chopped onion, diced carrots, and diced celery until softened. Add minced garlic and cook until fragrant.
4. Stir in diced tomatoes, dried thyme, dried rosemary, salt, and pepper. Add the cooked lentils and mix well.
5. Transfer the lentil mixture to a baking dish.
6. In a separate pot, boil diced potatoes until tender. Mash them with almond milk and vegan butter.

7. Spread the mashed potatoes over the lentil mixture in the baking dish.
8. Bake for 20-25 minutes until the top is golden brown.
9. Serve this comforting Lentil Shepherd's Pie prepared with your Tower Dual Basket Air Fryer.

Teriyaki Beef Skewers

Prep Time: 15 minutes / Cook Time: 15 minutes / Servings: 4 / Mode: Roast

Ingredients:
- 500g beef sirloin, cut into cubes
- 1 tablespoon vegetable oil
- 1 red onion, cut into chunks
- 120ml teriyaki sauce
- 1 bell pepper, cut into chunks
- Bamboo skewers, soaked in water

Preparation Instructions:
1. Preheat the air fryer to 400°F in Roast mode.
2. Marinate beef cubes in teriyaki sauce for at least 10 minutes.
3. Thread marinated beef, bell pepper, and red onion alternately onto the soaked bamboo skewers.
4. Brush vegetable oil over the skewers.
5. Roast the skewers for 12-15 minutes, turning occasionally, until the beef is cooked to your liking.
6. Serve these flavourful Teriyaki Beef Skewers for a delicious and easy meal.

Thai Green Curry with Tofu

Prep Time: 20 minutes / Cook Time: 25 minutes / Servings: 4 / Mode: Air Fry

Ingredients:
- 200g firm tofu, cubed
- 1 tablespoon vegetable oil
- 100g bamboo shoots
- 1 can (400ml) coconut milk
- 1 bell pepper, sliced
- Fresh basil leaves for garnish
- 2 tablespoons green curry paste
- 1 zucchini, sliced
- Cooked jasmine rice for serving

Preparation Instructions:
1. Preheat the air fryer to 375°F in Air Fry mode.
2. In a pan, heat vegetable oil and sauté green curry paste until fragrant.
3. Add cubed tofu and stir until lightly browned.
4. Pour in coconut milk, bell pepper, zucchini, and bamboo shoots. Simmer until vegetables are tender.
5. Air fry the Thai Green Curry for an additional 5-7 minutes for enhanced flavours.
6. Garnish with fresh basil leaves and serve over cooked jasmine rice.

Mushroom and Spinach Stuffed Peppers

Prep Time: 20 minutes / Cook Time: 25 minutes / Servings: 4 / Mode: Bake

Ingredients:
- 4 bell peppers, halved and seeds removed
- 150g fresh spinach, chopped
- 30ml olive oil
- Salt and pepper to taste
- 1 onion, finely chopped
- 200g cooked quinoa
- 200g mushrooms, chopped
- 2 cloves garlic, minced
- 100g feta cheese, crumbled

Preparation Instructions:
1. Preheat the air fryer to 375°F in Bake mode.
2. In a pan, sauté chopped mushrooms, spinach, chopped onion, and minced garlic in olive oil until vegetables are tender.
3. In a bowl, mix sautéed vegetables with cooked quinoa and crumbled feta cheese. Season with salt and pepper.
4. Stuff each bell pepper half with the quinoa mixture.

5. Bake for 20-25 minutes until the peppers are tender.
6. Serve hot and enjoy.

Chicken Pesto Pasta

Prep Time: 15 minutes / Cook Time: 20 minutes / Servings: 4 / Mode: Roast

Ingredients:
- 400g chicken breasts, sliced
- 50g pine nuts, toasted
- Salt and pepper to taste
- 300g penne pasta, cooked
- 75g pesto sauce
- Fresh basil leaves for garnish
- 150g cherry tomatoes, halved
- 30ml olive oil

Preparation Instructions:
1. Preheat the air fryer to 400°F in Roast mode.
2. Season sliced chicken breasts with salt and pepper. Roast for 15-20 minutes until cooked through.
3. In a large bowl, combine cooked penne pasta, roasted chicken, cherry tomatoes, toasted pine nuts, and pesto sauce. Drizzle olive oil and toss until well coated.
4. Garnish with fresh basil leaves before serving.

Baked Ziti

Prep Time: 15 minutes / Cook Time: 30 minutes / Servings: 6 / Mode: Bake

Ingredients:
- 400g ziti pasta, cooked
- 150g mozzarella cheese, shredded
- 1 egg, beaten
- Fresh basil for garnish
- 500ml marinara sauce
- 1 teaspoon dried oregano
- 250g ricotta cheese
- 50g Parmesan cheese, grated
- Salt and pepper to taste

Preparation Instructions:
1. Preheat the air fryer to 375°F in Bake mode.
2. In a large bowl, combine cooked ziti pasta with marinara sauce, ricotta cheese, half of the mozzarella cheese, Parmesan cheese, beaten egg, dried oregano, salt, and pepper.
3. Transfer the mixture to a baking dish and sprinkle the remaining mozzarella cheese on top.
4. Bake for 25-30 minutes until the cheese is melted and bubbly.
5. Garnish with fresh basil before serving.

Salmon en Papillote

Prep Time: 10 minutes / Cook Time: 20 minutes / Servings: 4 / Mode: Roast

Ingredients:
- 4 salmon fillets
- 4 sprigs fresh dill
- 200g cherry tomatoes, halved
- 30ml olive oil
- 1 lemon, thinly sliced
- Salt and pepper to taste

Preparation Instructions:
1. Preheat the air fryer to 400°F in Roast mode.
2. Place each salmon fillet on a piece of parchment paper. Season with salt and pepper.
3. Top each fillet with cherry tomatoes, lemon slices, and a sprig of fresh dill. Drizzle with olive oil.
4. Fold the parchment paper to create packets and place them in the air fryer basket.
5. Roast for 18-20 minutes until the salmon is cooked through.
6. Serve this elegant Salmon en Papillote for the best family dinner time.

Cod with Chorizo and Potatoes

Prep Time: 15 minutes / Cook Time: 25 minutes / Servings: 4 / Mode: Roast

Ingredients:

- 4 cod fillets
- 1 onion, finely chopped
- 1 teaspoon smoked paprika
- 200g chorizo, sliced
- 2 cloves garlic, minced
- Salt and pepper to taste
- 500g baby potatoes, halved
- 30ml olive oil
- Fresh parsley for garnish

Preparation Instructions:

1. Preheat the air fryer to 400°F in Roast mode.
2. In a bowl, toss the baby potatoes with olive oil, smoked paprika, salt, and pepper. Place them in the air fryer basket.
3. Roast the potatoes for 15 minutes, then add sliced chorizo and roast for an additional 5 minutes.
4. Season the cod fillets with salt and pepper. Place them on top of the chorizo and potatoes.
5. Roast for another 5-7 minutes until the cod is cooked through.
6. Garnish with fresh parsley before serving.

Chicken and Mushroom Stroganoff

Prep Time: 10 minutes / Cook Time: 20 minutes / Servings: 4 / Mode: Bake

Ingredients:

- 500g chicken breast, thinly sliced
- 2 cloves garlic, minced
- 30g butter
- Fresh parsley for garnish
- 200g mushrooms, sliced
- 200ml chicken broth
- 30ml olive oil
- 1 onion, finely chopped
- 150ml sour cream
- Salt and pepper to taste

Preparation Instructions:

1. Preheat the air fryer to 375°F in Bake mode.
2. In the air fryer pan, heat olive oil and sauté sliced chicken until browned.
3. Add chopped onion and mushrooms, continue baking until vegetables are softened.
4. Stir in minced garlic and bake for an additional minute.
5. Pour in chicken broth and let it bake for 5 minutes.
6. Add sour cream, butter, salt, and pepper. Stir until well combined and creamy.
7. Garnish with fresh parsley before serving.

Spinach and Ricotta Stuffed Chicken Breast

Prep Time: 15 minutes / Cook Time: 25 minutes / Servings: 4 / Mode: Roast

Ingredients:

- 4 chicken breasts
- 2 cloves garlic, minced
- Lemon wedges for serving
- 200g fresh spinach, chopped
- 30ml olive oil
- 150g ricotta cheese
- Salt and pepper to taste

Preparation Instructions:

1. Preheat the air fryer to 375°F in Roast mode.
2. In a bowl, mix chopped spinach, ricotta cheese, minced garlic, salt, and pepper.
3. Create a pocket in each chicken breast by slicing horizontally. Stuff the pockets with the spinach and ricotta mixture.
4. Brush each stuffed chicken breast with olive oil.
5. Roast in the air fryer for 25 minutes or until the chicken is cooked through.
6. Serve with lemon wedges for a delightful Spinach and Ricotta Stuffed Chicken Breast.

Steak Diane

Prep Time: 10 minutes / Cook Time: 15 minutes / Servings: 2 / Mode: Air Fry

Ingredients:

- 2 beef tenderloin steaks
- 100ml beef broth
- 2 tablespoons butter
- 50g mushrooms, sliced
- 30ml heavy cream
- Salt and pepper to taste
- 2 tablespoons brandy
- 1 tablespoon Dijon mustard
- Chopped parsley for garnish

Preparation Instructions:

1. Preheat the air fryer to 400°F in Air Fry mode.
2. Season the beef tenderloin steaks with salt and pepper.
3. Air fry the steaks for 10-12 minutes, turning halfway through, until desired doneness.
4. In a pan, sauté sliced mushrooms with butter until tender.
5. Pour in brandy and let it cook off, then add beef broth, heavy cream, and Dijon mustard. Simmer until the sauce thickens.
6. Serve the air-fried steaks with the Mushroom and Brandy Sauce, garnished with chopped parsley.

Baked Chicken with Honey Mustard Glaze

Prep Time: 15 minutes / Cook Time: 30 minutes / Servings: 4 / Mode: Bake

Ingredients:

- 4 boneless, skinless chicken breasts (about 600g)
- 30ml honey
- 30ml olive oil
- 1 teaspoon dried thyme
- Salt and pepper to taste
- 60ml Dijon mustard
- 2 cloves garlic, minced

Preparation Instructions:

1. Preheat the Air Fryer to 375°F in Bake mode.
2. In a bowl, mix Dijon mustard, honey, olive oil, minced garlic, dried thyme, salt, and pepper.
3. Place the chicken breasts in a baking dish and brush them with the honey mustard glaze.
4. Bake for 25-30 minutes or until the chicken is cooked through, basting with the glaze halfway through.
5. Serve the Baked Chicken with Honey Mustard Glaze with your favorite sides.

Chicken Alfredo Pasta Bake

Prep Time: 20 minutes / Cook Time: 25 minutes / Servings: 6 / Mode: Bake

Ingredients:

- 400g penne pasta, cooked
- 90g broccoli florets, blanched
- 120g shredded mozzarella cheese
- Salt and pepper to taste
- 300g cooked chicken, shredded
- 1 jar (450g) Alfredo sauce
- 50g grated Parmesan cheese
- Chopped fresh parsley for garnish

Preparation Instructions:

1. Preheat the Air Fryer to 375°F in Bake mode.
2. In a large bowl, combine cooked pasta, shredded chicken, blanched broccoli, and Alfredo sauce. Season with salt and pepper.
3. Transfer the mixture to a baking dish and sprinkle mozzarella and Parmesan cheese on top.
4. Bake for 20-25 minutes or until the cheese is melted and bubbly.
5. Garnish with chopped fresh parsley and serve your delicious Chicken Alfredo Pasta Bake. Enjoy!

Beef, Pork and Lamb

Beef and Ale Pie

Prep Time: 20 minutes / Cook Time: 2 hours / Servings: 4 / Mode: Bake

Ingredients:

- 500g beef stew meat, diced
- 2 cloves garlic, minced
- 2 tablespoons tomato paste
- Salt and pepper to taste
- 1 onion, chopped
- 200ml ale
- 2 tablespoons flour
- Pastry dough for pie crust
- 2 carrots, sliced
- 200ml beef broth
- 1 teaspoon thyme

Preparation Instructions:

1. Preheat the Air Fryer to 375°F in Bake mode.
2. In a large Air Fryer-safe pot, brown the beef stew meat over medium heat.
3. Add chopped onion, sliced carrots, and minced garlic to the pot. Cook until the vegetables are softened.
4. Stir in ale, beef broth, tomato paste, flour, thyme, salt, and pepper. Bring to a simmer.
5. Cover the pot and transfer it to the preheated Air Fryer. Bake for 1.5 to 2 hours or until the beef is tender.
6. Roll out the pastry dough and cover the pot with it. Cut a few slits in the crust for ventilation.
7. Bake for an additional 20-25 minutes or until the crust is golden brown.
8. Allow the Beef and Ale Pie to cool slightly before serving.

Pork and Apple Pie

Prep Time: 15 minutes / Cook Time: 1.5 hours / Servings: 4 / Mode: Bake

Ingredients:

- 500g pork shoulder, diced
- 2 cloves garlic, minced
- 2 tablespoons flour
- Pastry dough for pie crust
- 2 apples, peeled and sliced
- 200ml apple cider
- 1 teaspoon sage
- 1 onion, chopped
- 200ml chicken broth
- Salt and pepper to taste

Preparation Instructions:

1. Preheat the Air Fryer to 375°F in Bake mode.
2. In a large Air Fryer-safe pot, brown the diced pork shoulder over medium heat.
3. Add chopped onion and minced garlic to the pot. Cook until the vegetables are softened.
4. Stir in apple slices, apple cider, chicken broth, flour, sage, salt, and pepper. Bring to a simmer.
5. Cover the pot and transfer it to the preheated Air Fryer. Bake for 1 to 1.5 hours or until the pork is cooked through.
6. Roll out the pastry dough and cover the pot with it. Cut a few slits in the crust for ventilation.
7. Bake for an additional 20-25 minutes or until the crust is golden brown.
8. Allow the Pork and Apple Pie to cool slightly before serving.

Herb-Crusted Rack of Lamb

Prep Time: 15 minutes / Cook Time: 30 minutes / Servings: 2 / Mode: Roast

Ingredients:

- 1 rack of lamb (about 500g)
- 2 tablespoons fresh breadcrumbs
- 1 tablespoon fresh rosemary, chopped
- 2 cloves garlic, minced
- 2 tablespoons Dijon mustard
- 1 tablespoon fresh parsley, chopped
- 1 tablespoon fresh thyme, chopped
- Salt and black pepper to taste

- Olive oil for searing

Preparation Instructions:

1. Preheat the Air Fryer to 400°F in Roast mode.
2. Season the rack of lamb with salt and black pepper.
3. In a small bowl, mix Dijon mustard, breadcrumbs, chopped parsley, rosemary, thyme, and minced garlic to create the herb crust.
4. Heat olive oil in an Air Fryer-safe skillet over medium-high heat.
5. Sear the lamb rack on all sides until browned.
6. Remove the lamb from the heat and spread the herb crust evenly over the meat.
7. Place the skillet in the preheated Air Fryer and roast for about 20-25 minutes for medium-rare or adjust to your desired doneness.
8. Allow the Herb-Crusted Rack of Lamb to rest for a few minutes before slicing.

Paprika Pork Goulash

Prep Time: 20 minutes / Cook Time: 1.5 hours / Servings: 4 / Mode: Roast

Ingredients:

- 500g pork shoulder, diced
- 2 tablespoons sweet paprika
- 400g canned tomatoes, crushed
- Olive oil for cooking
- 2 onions, finely chopped
- 1 teaspoon caraway seeds
- 300ml beef broth
- 2 red bell peppers, sliced
- 2 cloves garlic, minced
- Salt and black pepper to taste

Preparation Instructions:

1. Preheat the Air Fryer to 350°F in Roast mode.
2. In an Air Fryer-safe pot, heat olive oil over medium heat. Add diced pork and brown on all sides.
3. Add chopped onions and sliced red bell peppers. Cook until softened.
4. Stir in sweet paprika, caraway seeds, and minced garlic. Cook for another 2 minutes.
5. Pour in crushed tomatoes and beef broth. Season with salt and black pepper. Bring to a simmer.
6. Cover the pot and transfer it to the preheated Air Fryer. Roast for 1 to 1.5 hours or until the pork is tender.
7. Serve the Paprika Pork Goulash over rice or with crusty bread.

Beef and Cheddar Stuffed Peppers

Prep Time: 15 minutes / Cook Time: 25 minutes / Servings: 4 / Mode: Air Fry

Ingredients:

- 4 large bell peppers, halved and seeds removed
- 1 onion, finely chopped
- 180g cooked quinoa
- Salt and black pepper to taste
- 2 cloves garlic, minced
- 1 teaspoon ground cumin
- Olive oil for cooking
- 500g lean ground beef
- 200g cheddar cheese, shredded
- 1 teaspoon paprika

Preparation Instructions:

1. Preheat the air fryer to 375°F in Air Fry mode.
2. In a skillet, heat olive oil over medium heat. Add chopped onions and garlic. Cook until softened.
3. Add ground beef and cook until browned. Drain excess fat if needed.
4. Season the beef with ground cumin, paprika, salt, and black pepper.
5. In a large bowl, mix the cooked beef with cooked quinoa and shredded cheddar cheese.
6. Stuff each bell pepper half with the beef and quinoa mixture.
7. Place the stuffed peppers in the air fryer basket.
8. Air fry for about 20-25 minutes until the peppers are tender and the filling is heated through.
9. Serve the Beef and Cheddar Stuffed Peppers hot.

Lamb Curry

Prep Time: 20 minutes / Cook Time: 35 minutes / Servings: 4 / Mode: Roast

Ingredients:

- 500g lamb, cubed
- 3 cloves garlic, minced
- 1 teaspoon ground turmeric
- Fresh coriander for garnish
- 2 onions, finely chopped
- 1-inch ginger, grated
- 1 teaspoon ground cumin
- 3 tomatoes, chopped
- 2 tablespoons curry powder
- 400ml coconut milk
- Salt and vegetable oil for cooking

Preparation Instructions:

1. Preheat the air fryer to 375°F in Roast mode.
2. In a pan, heat vegetable oil over medium heat. Add chopped onions and cook until golden brown.
3. Add minced garlic, grated ginger, curry powder, ground turmeric, and ground cumin. Cook for 2 minutes.
4. Stir in cubed lamb and cook until browned.
5. Add chopped tomatoes and coconut milk. Season with salt.
6. Transfer the lamb curry to the air fryer basket.
7. Roast for about 30-35 minutes, stirring occasionally, until the lamb is tender.
8. Garnish with fresh coriander before serving.
9. Enjoy the aromatic and flavourful Lamb Curry from your air fryer!

Pork and Sage Meatballs

Prep Time: 15 minutes / Cook Time: 20 minutes / Servings: 4 / Mode: Air Fry

Ingredients:

- 500g ground pork
- 2 tablespoons fresh sage, finely chopped
- 60g breadcrumbs
- Salt and pepper to taste
- 1 egg
- Olive oil for brushing

Preparation Instructions:

1. In a bowl, combine 500g ground pork, 60g breadcrumbs, 1 egg, chopped sage, salt, and pepper.
2. Shape the mixture into meatballs.
3. Preheat the air fryer to 375°F in Air Fry mode.
4. Brush the meatballs with olive oil.
5. Air fry for 15-20 minutes, turning halfway through, until golden brown and cooked through.
6. Serve the Pork and Sage Meatballs hot.

Beef Burritos

Prep Time: 20 minutes / Cook Time: 15 minutes / Servings: 4 / Mode: Roast

Ingredients:

- 500g ground beef
- 1 tablespoon taco seasoning
- 4 large flour tortillas
- Salsa and guacamole for serving
- 1 onion, diced
- 200g cooked black beans
- 100g shredded cheddar cheese
- 2 cloves garlic, minced
- 200g cooked rice

Preparation Instructions:

1. In a pan, cook 500g ground beef, diced onion, and minced garlic until browned. Add taco seasoning.
2. Stir in 200g black beans and 200g cooked rice.
3. Preheat the air fryer to 400°F in Roast mode.
4. Place a portion of the beef mixture onto each tortilla, top with 100g shredded cheddar.
5. Roll and place the burritos in the air fryer. Roast for about 10-15 minutes until the tortillas are crispy.
6. Serve the Beef Burritos with salsa and guacamole.

Rosemary and Garlic Pork Roast

Prep Time: 15 minutes / Cook Time: 45 minutes / Servings: 4 / Mode: Roast

Ingredients:
- 800g pork loin roast
- 3 cloves garlic, minced
- 2 tablespoons fresh rosemary, chopped
- Salt and pepper to taste
- 30ml olive oil

Preparation Instructions:
1. Preheat the air fryer to 375°F in Roast mode.
2. In a small bowl, mix minced garlic, chopped rosemary, salt, pepper, and olive oil.
3. Rub the garlic and rosemary mixture all over the pork roast.
4. Place the pork roast in the air fryer basket.
5. Roast for 40-45 minutes or until the internal temperature reaches 145°F, turning halfway through.
6. Let the Rosemary and Garlic Pork Roast rest for a few minutes before slicing.

Lamb Chops with Balsamic Reduction

Prep Time: 10 minutes / Cook Time: 15 minutes / Servings: 4 / Mode: Air Fry

Ingredients:
- 8 lamb chops
- Salt and pepper to taste
- 60ml balsamic vinegar
- 30ml olive oil
- 1 tablespoon fresh mint, chopped

Preparation Instructions:
1. Preheat the air fryer to 400°F in Air Fry mode.
2. Season lamb chops with salt and pepper.
3. In a small saucepan, heat balsamic vinegar over low heat until reduced by half.
4. Brush lamb chops with olive oil.
5. Air fry lamb chops for about 12-15 minutes, turning once, until desired doneness.
6. Drizzle balsamic reduction over the lamb chops and sprinkle with fresh mint before serving.

Korean BBQ Beef Short Ribs

Prep Time: 20 minutes / Cook Time: 15 minutes / Servings: 4 / Mode: Air Fry

Ingredients:
- 1 kg beef short ribs, cut into individual pieces
- 120ml soy sauce
- 60ml mirin
- 60ml brown sugar
- 3 cloves garlic, minced
- 1 tablespoon sesame oil
- 1 tablespoon grated ginger
- 2 green onions, chopped
- Sesame seeds for garnish

Preparation Instructions:
1. Preheat the air fryer to 375°F in Air Fry mode.
2. In a bowl, whisk together soy sauce, mirin, brown sugar, minced garlic, sesame oil, and grated ginger to create the marinade.
3. Place the beef short ribs in a zip-top bag and pour the marinade over them. Seal the bag and let it marinate in the refrigerator for at least 1 hour.
4. Remove the short ribs from the marinade and place them in the air fryer basket, ensuring they are not crowded.
5. Air fry for 12-15 minutes, turning halfway through, until the ribs are caramelised and cooked to your liking.
6. Garnish with chopped green onions and sesame seeds before serving.

Fried Pork with Broccoli

Prep Time: 15 minutes / Cook Time: 15 minutes / Servings: 4 / Mode: Fry

Ingredients:

- 500g pork tenderloin, thinly sliced
- 60ml soy sauce
- 15ml hoisin sauce
- 1 broccoli head, cut into florets
- Salt and pepper to taste
- 30ml oyster sauce
- 2 tablespoons vegetable oi
- Sesame seeds for garnish
- 60g cornstarch
- 15ml rice vinegar
- 3 cloves garlic, minced

Preparation Instructions:

1. In a bowl, season pork slices with salt and pepper. Coat each slice with cornstarch.
2. In a separate bowl, whisk together soy sauce, oyster sauce, rice vinegar, and hoisin sauce to create the sauce.
3. Heat vegetable oil in a pan or wok over medium-high heat. Add pork slices and stir-fry until golden brown and cooked through.
4. Remove pork from the pan and set aside.
5. In the same pan, add a bit more oil if needed. Stir-fry broccoli and minced garlic until the broccoli is tender-crisp.
6. Return the cooked pork to the pan and pour the sauce over the pork and broccoli. Toss everything together until well coated.
7. Garnish with sesame seeds before serving.

Greek-style Lamb Souvlaki

Prep Time: 20 minutes / Cook Time: 10 minutes / Servings: 4 / Mode: Roast

Ingredients:

- 500g lamb leg, cubed
- 1 teaspoon dried oregano
- Salt and pepper to taste
- 2 tablespoons olive oil
- 1 teaspoon ground cumin
- 4 pita bread
- 3 cloves garlic, minced
- Juice of 1 lemon
- Tzatziki sauce and sliced tomatoes for serving

Preparation Instructions:

1. In a bowl, combine olive oil, minced garlic, dried oregano, ground cumin, lemon juice, salt, and pepper to create the marinade.
2. Add the cubed lamb to the marinade, ensuring each piece is well coated. Allow it to marinate for at least 15 minutes.
3. Thread the marinated lamb onto skewers.
4. Preheat the Air Fryer to medium-high heat.
5. Roast the lamb skewers for about 8-10 minutes, turning occasionally, until the lamb is cooked to your liking.
6. Warm the pita bread on the grill for a minute on each side.
7. Serve the lamb souvlaki in the pita bread, topped with tzatziki sauce and sliced tomatoes.

Korean Beef Bulgogi

Prep Time: 15 minutes / Cook Time: 10 minutes / Servings: 4 / Mode: Air Fry

Ingredients:

- 500g beef sirloin, thinly sliced
- 1 tablespoon sesame oil
- 2 green onions, chopped
- 60ml soy sauce
- 3 cloves garlic, minced
- Sesame seeds for garnish
- 2 tablespoons brown sugar
- 1 teaspoon grated ginger

Preparation Instructions:

1. In a bowl, whisk together soy sauce, brown sugar, sesame oil, minced garlic, and grated ginger to create the marinade.
2. Add the thinly sliced beef to the marinade and let it marinate for at least 15 minutes.
3. Preheat the air fryer to 400°F in Air Fry mode.
4. Place the marinated beef in the air fryer basket and cook for about 10 minutes or until browned and cooked through.

5. Sprinkle chopped green onions and sesame seeds over the beef before serving.
6. Serve the Korean Beef Bulgogi over rice or with your favorite side dishes.

Pork Schnitzel

Prep Time: 20 minutes / Cook Time: 15 minutes / Servings: 4 / Mode: Bake

Ingredients:
- 4 pork loin chops, boneless
- 150g breadcrumbs
- 100g all-purpose flour
- Salt and pepper to taste
- 2 large eggs, beaten
- Cooking spray

Preparation Instructions:
1. Preheat the air fryer to 375°F in Bake mode.
2. Season the pork loin chops with salt and pepper.
3. Dredge each chop in flour, dip into beaten eggs, and coat with breadcrumbs.
4. Place the breaded pork chops in the air fryer basket.
5. Bake for about 15 minutes, turning halfway through, until the pork is golden brown and cooked through.
6. Serve the Pork Schnitzel with your choice of sides and enjoy a delightful meal.

Spicy Beef Tacos

Prep Time: 15 minutes / Cook Time: 10 minutes / Servings: 4 / Mode: Air Fry

Ingredients:
- 500g beef, minced
- 1 teaspoon smoked paprika
- 8 small corn tortillas
- 1 tablespoon Chilli powder
- 1/2 teaspoon cayenne pepper
- Toppings: salsa, guacamole, shredded lettuce, shredded cheese
- 1 teaspoon cumin
- Salt and pepper to taste

Preparation Instructions:
1. In a skillet, cook minced beef over medium heat until browned.
2. Add Chilli powder, cumin, smoked paprika, cayenne pepper, salt, and pepper to the beef. Cook for an additional 5 minutes, allowing the flavours to meld.
3. Preheat the air fryer to 375°F in Air Fry mode.
4. Place corn tortillas in the air fryer basket and cook for 2-3 minutes until they become crispy.
5. Fill each tortilla with the spicy beef mixture.
6. Top with salsa, guacamole, shredded lettuce, and cheese.
7. Serve these Spicy Beef Tacos for a zesty and satisfying meal.

Pork Carnitas

Prep Time: 20 minutes / Cook Time: 15 minutes / Servings: 4 / Mode: Roast

Ingredients:
- 800g pork shoulder, diced
- 1 teaspoon dried oregano
- Corn or flour tortillas
- 1 tablespoon olive oil
- 1 teaspoon smoked paprika
- Toppings: diced onions, cilantro, lime wedges
- 1 teaspoon ground cumin
- Salt and pepper to taste

Preparation Instructions:
1. Preheat the air fryer to 400°F in Roast mode.
2. In a bowl, toss diced pork shoulder with olive oil, ground cumin, dried oregano, smoked paprika, salt, and pepper.
3. Place the seasoned pork in the air fryer basket.
4. Roast for about 15 minutes, turning the pork halfway through, until it becomes golden and crispy.
5. Warm tortillas in the air fryer for 2 minutes.
6. Serve the Pork Carnitas in warm tortillas and top with diced onions, cilantro, and lime wedges.

Beef Rouladen

Prep Time: 20 minutes / Cook Time: 30 minutes / Servings: 4 / Mode: Roast

Ingredients:
- 4 beef round steaks
- 4 dill pickles, sliced
- 2 tablespoons vegetable oil
- 4 slices bacon
- Mustard to taste
- 500ml beef broth
- 1 onion, finely chopped
- Salt and pepper to taste
- 2 tablespoons flour

Preparation Instructions:
1. Preheat the air fryer to 400°F in Roast mode.
2. Lay out the beef round steaks and spread mustard on each one. Season with salt and pepper.
3. Place a slice of bacon, chopped onion, and a dill pickle slice on each steak.
4. Roll up the steaks and secure with toothpicks.
5. In a bowl, mix flour with a bit of water to form a paste.
6. Heat vegetable oil in the air fryer basket. Brown the beef rolls on all sides.
7. Pour beef broth over the beef rouladen and brush with the flour paste.
8. Roast for about 30 minutes until the beef is cooked through.
9. Serve the Beef Rouladen with the savory gravy.

Pulled Pork Tamales

Prep Time: 30 minutes / Cook Time: 1 hour / Servings: 4 / Mode: Air Fry

Ingredients:
- 380g pulled pork
- 5g baking powder
- 115g lard or vegetable shortening
- 250g masa harina
- Salt to taste
- 350ml chicken broth
- Corn husks, soaked in warm water

Preparation Instructions:
1. Preheat the air fryer to 375°F in Air Fry mode.
2. In a bowl, mix masa harina, chicken broth, lard or shortening, baking powder, and salt to form a smooth dough.
3. Spread a thin layer of masa on each corn husk.
4. Place a spoonful of pulled pork in the center and roll the tamale, securing the ends.
5. Arrange tamales in the air fryer basket, standing them upright.
6. Air fry for about 1 hour until the masa is cooked through.
7. Serve the Pulled Pork Tamales with your favorite toppings.

Greek-style Lamb Gyros

Prep Time: 15 minutes / Cook Time: 20 minutes / Servings: 4 / Mode: Air Fry

Ingredients:
- 500g boneless lamb, thinly sliced
- 2 cloves garlic, minced
- 4 pita bread
- 2 tablespoons olive oil
- 1 teaspoon dried oregano
- Tzatziki sauce, tomatoes, cucumbers, and red onions for serving
- 1 tablespoon red wine vinegar
- Salt and pepper to taste

Preparation Instructions:
1. Preheat the air fryer to 375°F in Air Fry mode.
2. In a bowl, mix olive oil, red wine vinegar, minced garlic, dried oregano, salt, and pepper.
3. Toss the thinly sliced lamb in the marinade and let it sit for at least 10 minutes.
4. Air fry the marinated lamb slices for about 15-20 minutes until cooked through and slightly crispy.
5. Warm the pita bread in the air fryer for a few seconds.
6. Assemble the gyros by placing the cooked lamb on the pita bread and topping with tzatziki sauce, tomatoes, cucumbers, and red onions.

7. Serve the Greek-style Lamb Gyros for a delicious and flavourful meal.

Pork Tenderloin Medallions with Mustard Sauce

Prep Time: 15 minutes / Cook Time: 25 minutes / Servings: 4 / Mode: Roast

Ingredients:
- 600g pork tenderloin, sliced into medallions
- 2 tablespoons olive oil
- 120ml chicken broth
- 2 tablespoons heavy cream
- Fresh parsley for garnish
- Salt and pepper to taste
- 2 tablespoons Dijon mustard

Preparation Instructions:
1. Preheat the air fryer to 400°F in Roast mode.
2. Season pork tenderloin medallions with salt and pepper.
3. Heat olive oil in the air fryer basket and sear the pork medallions until golden brown on both sides.
4. In a bowl, whisk together chicken broth, Dijon mustard, and heavy cream.
5. Pour the mustard sauce over the pork medallions in the air fryer basket.
6. Roast for about 20-25 minutes until the pork is cooked through and the sauce thickens.
7. Garnish with fresh parsley and serve the Pork Tenderloin Medallions with Mustard Sauce.

Vietnamese Lemongrass Beef

Prep Time: 20 minutes / Cook Time: 15 minutes / Servings: 4 / Mode: Air Fry

Ingredients:
- 500g beef sirloin, thinly sliced
- 1 tablespoon brown sugar
- 3 cloves garlic, minced
- 2 tablespoons vegetable oil
- 3 tablespoons soy sauce
- 2 tablespoons lemongrass, minced
- 1 red chilli, sliced
- Fresh cilantro and lime wedges for serving
- 2 tablespoons fish sauce

Preparation Instructions:
1. Preheat the air fryer to 375°F in Air Fry mode.
2. In a bowl, mix soy sauce, fish sauce, brown sugar, minced lemongrass, minced garlic, and sliced red Chilli.
3. Toss the thinly sliced beef in the lemongrass marinade and let it sit for at least 15 minutes.
4. Heat vegetable oil in the air fryer basket and cook the marinated beef for about 10-15 minutes until cooked through and slightly charred.
5. Serve the Vietnamese Lemongrass Beef with fresh cilantro and lime wedges.

Pork and Apple Stuffed Squash

Prep Time: 20 minutes / Cook Time: 30 minutes / Servings: 4 / Mode: Roast

Ingredients:
- 2 acorn squash, halved and seeds removed
- 1 onion, diced
- 2 teaspoons sage
- 2 apples, peeled and diced
- Salt and pepper to taste
- 400g ground pork
- 115g breadcrumbs
- 2 tablespoons olive oil

Preparation Instructions:
1. Preheat the air fryer to 400°F in Roast mode.
2. Place acorn squash halves in the air fryer basket.
3. In a skillet, cook ground pork, diced onion, diced apples, breadcrumbs, sage, salt, and pepper until pork is browned.
4. Stuff each acorn squash half with the pork and apple mixture.
5. Drizzle olive oil over the stuffed squash.
6. Roast for about 25-30 minutes until the squash is tender.
7. Serve the Pork and Apple Stuffed Squash as a delightful and comforting meal.

Fish and Seafood

Baked Scallops with Garlic and Lemon

Prep Time: 15 minutes / Cook Time: 12 minutes / Servings: 4 / Mode: Bake

Ingredients:

- 500g scallops
- 2 tablespoons olive oil
- 3 cloves garlic, minced
- Salt and pepper to taste
- Zest of 1 lemon
- Fresh parsley for garnish

Preparation Instructions:

1. Preheat the air fryer to 375°F in Bake mode.
2. In a bowl, combine scallops, minced garlic, lemon zest, olive oil, salt, and pepper. Toss to coat evenly.
3. Place the scallops in the air fryer basket.
4. Bake for 10-12 minutes until the scallops are opaque and cooked through.
5. Garnish with fresh parsley before serving.
6. Enjoy these delightful Baked Scallops with Garlic and Lemon as a flavourful seafood dish.

Mediterranean Stuffed Squid

Prep Time: 20 minutes / Cook Time: 20 minutes / Servings: 4 / Mode: Roast

Ingredients:

- 4 medium-sized squid tubes
- 50g Kalamata olives, sliced
- Salt and pepper to taste
- 200g cherry tomatoes, halved
- 2 tablespoons olive oil
- 100g feta cheese, crumbled
- 1 teaspoon dried oregano

Preparation Instructions:

1. Preheat the air fryer to 400°F in Roast mode.
2. In a bowl, mix cherry tomatoes, feta cheese, Kalamata olives, olive oil, dried oregano, salt, and pepper.
3. Stuff the squid tubes with the Mediterranean mixture.
4. Place the stuffed squid in the air fryer basket.
5. Roast for 18-20 minutes until the squid is cooked and the filling is heated through.
6. Serve these flavourful Mediterranean Stuffed Squid as a delightful seafood dish.

Salmon Teriyaki Bowl

Prep Time: 15 minutes / Cook Time: 15 minutes / Servings: 4 / Mode: Air Fry

Ingredients:

- 4 salmon fillets
- 200g broccoli florets
- 120ml teriyaki sauce
- Sesame seeds for garnish
- 400g cooked jasmine rice
- Chopped green onions for garnish

Preparation Instructions:

1. Preheat the air fryer to 375°F in Air Fry mode.
2. Marinate salmon fillets in teriyaki sauce for at least 10 minutes.
3. Place marinated salmon in the air fryer basket.
4. Air fry for 12-15 minutes until salmon is cooked through.
5. Meanwhile, steam broccoli until tender.
6. Serve the salmon over cooked jasmine rice, top with steamed broccoli.

7. Garnish with sesame seeds and chopped green onions.

8. Enjoy this delicious Salmon Teriyaki Bowl as a wholesome and flavourful meal.

Cajun Shrimp Pasta

Prep Time: 15 minutes / Cook Time: 15 minutes / Servings: 4 / Mode: Roast

Ingredients:

- 400g shrimp, peeled and deveined
- 2 tablespoons Cajun seasoning
- 3 cloves garlic, minced
- Fresh parsley for garnish
- 200ml heavy cream
- Salt and pepper to taste
- 250g linguine pasta
- 2 tablespoons olive oil
- 100g cherry tomatoes, halved

Preparation Instructions:

1. Preheat the air fryer to 375°F in Roast mode.
2. Toss shrimp with Cajun seasoning in a bowl.
3. Cook linguine pasta according to package instructions.
4. In a pan, heat olive oil and sauté minced garlic until fragrant.
5. Add seasoned shrimp to the pan and roast in the air fryer for 6-8 minutes until cooked.
6. Pour heavy cream into the pan, add cherry tomatoes, and cook until the sauce thickens.
7. Toss the cooked pasta into the Cajun shrimp mixture.
8. Season with salt and pepper, garnish with fresh parsley.
9. Serve this flavourful Cajun Shrimp Pasta for a delightful pasta dish.

Pan-Fried Calamari

Prep Time: 20 minutes / Cook Time: 10 minutes / Servings: 4 / Mode: Air Fry

Ingredients:

- 300g squid tubes, cleaned and sliced into rings
- 2 teaspoons smoked paprika
- 1 teaspoon garlic powder
- Olive oil for frying
- Lemon wedges for serving
- 100g all-purpose flour
- Salt and pepper to taste

Preparation Instructions:

1. Preheat the air fryer to 375°F in Air Fry mode.
2. In a bowl, mix flour, smoked paprika, garlic powder, salt, and pepper.
3. Coat squid rings in the seasoned flour mixture.
4. Lightly spray or brush the squid rings with olive oil.
5. Air fry for 8-10 minutes until the calamari is crispy and golden.
6. Serve the Pan-Fried Calamari with lemon wedges for a tasty appetizer.

Pesto Grilled Shrimp Skewers

Prep Time: 15 minutes / Cook Time: 10 minutes / Servings: 4 / Mode: Roast

Ingredients:

- 400g large shrimp, peeled and deveined
- 1 lemon, juiced
- 2 cloves garlic, minced
- Wooden skewers, soaked in water
- 4 tablespoons pesto sauce
- Salt and pepper to taste

Preparation Instructions:

1. Preheat the air fryer to 400°F in Roast mode.
2. In a bowl, mix shrimp with pesto sauce, lemon juice, minced garlic, salt, and pepper.
3. Thread marinated shrimp onto soaked wooden skewers.
4. Roast in the air fryer for 8-10 minutes until the shrimp are opaque and grilled.

5. Serve these Pesto Grilled Shrimp Skewers for a flavourful and quick seafood dish.

Coconut Lime Grilled Tilapia

Prep Time: 15 minutes / Cook Time: 10 minutes / Servings: 4 / Mode: Roast

Ingredients:
- 4 tilapia fillets
- 2 teaspoons garlic powder
- Salt and pepper to taste
- 3 tablespoons coconut oil, melted
- 1 teaspoon paprika
- Fresh cilantro for garnish
- Zest and juice of 2 limes

Preparation Instructions:
1. Preheat the air fryer to 375°F in Roast mode.
2. In a bowl, mix melted coconut oil, lime zest, lime juice, garlic powder, paprika, salt, and pepper.
3. Brush the tilapia fillets with the coconut lime mixture.
4. Roast in the air fryer for 8-10 minutes until the tilapia is cooked through.
5. Garnish with fresh cilantro and serve these Coconut Lime Grilled Tilapia fillets.

Mussels in White Wine Garlic Sauce

Prep Time: 10 minutes / Cook Time: 10 minutes / Servings: 4 / Mode: Roast

Ingredients:
- 1 kg fresh mussels, cleaned and debearded
- 4 cloves garlic, minced
- Fresh parsley for garnish
- 240ml dry white wine
- Salt and pepper to taste
- 2 tablespoons olive oil
- 120ml chicken broth

Preparation Instructions:
1. Preheat the air fryer to 400°F in Roast mode.
2. In a pan, heat olive oil and sauté minced garlic until fragrant.
3. Add white wine and chicken broth to the pan, then bring to a simmer.
4. Add cleaned mussels to the pan, cover, and roast in the air fryer for 8-10 minutes until the mussels open.
5. Discard any unopened mussels, garnish with fresh parsley, and serve these Mussels in White Wine Garlic Sauce.

Blackened Catfish

Prep Time: 15 minutes / Cook Time: 10 minutes / Servings: 4 / Mode: Roast

Ingredients:
- 4 catfish fillets
- 1 teaspoon onion powder
- 1/2 teaspoon cayenne pepper
- 2 teaspoons paprika
- 1 teaspoon garlic powder
- Salt and pepper to taste
- 1 teaspoon dried thyme
- Olive oil for brushing

Preparation Instructions:
1. Preheat the air fryer to 380°F in Roast mode.
2. In a bowl, mix paprika, dried thyme, onion powder, garlic powder, cayenne pepper, salt, and pepper.
3. Brush catfish fillets with olive oil and coat them with the blackened spice mixture.
4. Roast in the air fryer for 8-10 minutes until the catfish is blackened and cooked through.
5. Serve this flavourful Blackened Catfish for a delicious seafood dish.

Roasted Lobster with Garlic Herb Butter

Prep Time: 15 minutes / Cook Time: 10 minutes / Servings: 2 / Mode: Grill

Ingredients:

- 2 lobster tails, split in half
- 3 cloves garlic, minced
- Salt and pepper to taste
- Lemon wedges for serving
- 4 tablespoons unsalted butter, melted
- 1 tablespoon fresh parsley, chopped

Preparation Instructions:

1. Preheat the Air Fryer.
2. In a bowl, mix melted butter, minced garlic, chopped parsley, salt, and pepper.
3. Brush the lobster tails with the garlic herb butter mixture.
4. Place the lobster tails on the preheated grill, shell side down. Grill for about 5 minutes.
5. Flip the lobster tails and brush with more garlic herb butter. Grill for an additional 5 minutes or until the lobster meat is opaque.
6. Serve the grilled lobster with lemon wedges.

Spicy Roasted Octopus

Prep Time: 15 minutes / Cook Time: 10 minutes / Servings: 4 / Mode: Roast

Ingredients:

- 1 kg octopus, cleaned and tentacles separated
- 2 teaspoons smoked paprika
- Salt and pepper to taste
- 2 tablespoons olive oil
- 1 teaspoon cayenne pepper
- Lemon wedges for serving

Preparation Instructions:

1. Preheat the Air Fryer.
2. In a bowl, mix olive oil, smoked paprika, cayenne pepper, salt, and pepper.
3. Brush the octopus tentacles with the spicy olive oil mixture.
4. Place the octopus on the preheated air fryer. Roast for about 5 minutes on each side or until charred and cooked through.
5. Serve the spicy grilled octopus with lemon wedges.

Crab and Corn Chowder

Prep Time: 15 minutes / Cook Time: 25 minutes / Servings: 4 / Mode: Air Fry

Ingredients:

- 200g lump crabmeat
- 2 potatoes, diced
- 2 tablespoons butter
- Fresh parsley for garnish
- 240ml corn kernels
- 720ml chicken broth
- 2 tablespoons all-purpose flour
- 1 onion, diced
- 240ml milk
- Salt and pepper to taste

Preparation Instructions:

1. In the air fryer, sauté diced onion and potatoes in butter until softened.
2. Sprinkle flour over the vegetables and stir to coat.
3. Pour in chicken broth and milk, stirring continuously to avoid lumps.
4. Add lump crabmeat and corn to the mixture. Season with salt and pepper.
5. Air fry for 25 minutes, stirring occasionally, until the chowder thickens and flavours meld.
6. Garnish with fresh parsley before serving.

Garlic Butter Shrimp Pasta

Prep Time: 10 minutes / Cook Time: 15 minutes / Servings: 4 / Mode: Roast

Ingredients:
- 300g linguine pasta
- 4 cloves garlic, minced
- 3 tablespoons butter
- Grated Parmesan cheese for serving
- 250g large shrimp, peeled and deveined
- 120ml cherry tomatoes, halved
- 2 tablespoons olive oil
- 60ml fresh parsley, chopped
- Salt and pepper to taste

Preparation Instructions:
1. Roast shrimp, garlic, and cherry tomatoes in the air fryer with olive oil for about 10-12 minutes until shrimp are pink and tomatoes are tender.
2. In the meantime, cook linguine pasta according to package instructions.
3. Toss the roasted shrimp mixture with cooked pasta.
4. Add butter and fresh parsley, season with salt and pepper.
5. Serve with a sprinkle of grated Parmesan cheese.

Seafood Paella

Prep Time: 20 minutes / Cook Time: 30 minutes / Servings: 4 / Mode: Roast

Ingredients:
- 250g bomba rice
- 200g mussels, cleaned
- 2 tomatoes, diced
- 1 teaspoon smoked paprika
- Salt and pepper to taste
- 500ml chicken broth
- 150g chorizo, sliced
- 2 cloves garlic, minced
- 200g shrimp, peeled and deveined
- 1 onion, diced
- 1 teaspoon saffron threads
- 2 tablespoons olive oil
- Lemon wedges for serving

Preparation Instructions:
1. Preheat the air fryer to 375°F in Roast mode.
2. In a large pan, sauté diced onion, garlic, and chorizo with olive oil until the onion is translucent.
3. Add bomba rice, diced tomatoes, saffron threads, and smoked paprika. Cook for a few minutes.
4. Pour in chicken broth and bring the mixture to a boil.
5. Transfer the mixture to the air fryer basket, arrange shrimp and mussels on top, and roast for 30 minutes until the rice is tender and seafood is cooked.
6. Season with salt and pepper, and serve with lemon wedges.

Lobster Mac and Cheese

Prep Time: 15 minutes / Cook Time: 20 minutes / Servings: 4 / Mode: Air Fry

Ingredients:
- 300g elbow macaroni
- 300ml milk
- 100g Gruyère cheese, shredded
- 3 tablespoons all-purpose flour
- Salt and pepper to taste
- 200g lobster meat, cooked and chopped
- 200g sharp cheddar cheese, shredded
- 3 tablespoons butter
- 1 teaspoon Dijon mustard
- Fresh parsley for garnish

Preparation Instructions:
1. Cook macaroni according to package instructions; drain and set aside.
2. In a saucepan, melt butter, stir in flour, and cook until golden.
3. Whisk in milk, Dijon mustard, and bring to a simmer.
4. Add shredded cheddar and Gruyère cheese, stirring until melted and smooth.

5. Fold in cooked macaroni and chopped lobster meat.
6. Transfer the mixture to the air fryer basket and air fry for 15-20 minutes until the top is golden and bubbly.
7. Garnish with fresh parsley and serve.

Baked Lemon Herb Tilapia

Prep Time: 10 minutes / Cook Time: 15 minutes / Servings: 4 / Mode: Bake

Ingredients:
- 4 tilapia fillets
- 2 cloves garlic, minced
- Salt and pepper to taste
- 2 tablespoons olive oil
- 1 teaspoon dried oregano
- Fresh parsley for garnish
- 1 lemon, juiced
- 1 teaspoon dried thyme

Preparation Instructions:
1. Preheat the air fryer to 375°F in Bake mode.
2. Place tilapia fillets in a baking dish.
3. In a bowl, mix olive oil, lemon juice, minced garlic, dried oregano, dried thyme, salt, and pepper.
4. Pour the mixture over tilapia fillets, ensuring they are well coated.
5. Bake for 15 minutes until the tilapia is cooked through and flakes easily with a fork.
6. Garnish with fresh parsley and serve.

Scallops with Brown Butter and Sage

Prep Time: 10 minutes / Cook Time: 10 minutes / Servings: 4 / Mode: Roast

Ingredients:
- 500g scallops
- Salt and pepper to taste
- 4 tablespoons unsalted butter
- Lemon wedges for serving
- Fresh sage leaves

Preparation Instructions:
1. Preheat the air fryer to 375°F in Roast mode.
2. Pat dry scallops with a paper towel and season with salt and pepper.
3. In a pan, melt butter over medium heat until it turns brown and develops a nutty aroma. Add fresh sage leaves during the last minute.
4. Place scallops in the air fryer basket and roast for about 5-7 minutes until they are cooked through and have a golden sear.
5. Drizzle brown butter and sage over the scallops.
6. Serve with lemon wedges and enjoy this elegant seafood dish.

Clam Linguine in White Wine Sauce

Prep Time: 15 minutes / Cook Time: 15 minutes / Servings: 4 / Mode: Roast

Ingredients:
- 400g linguine
- 2 tablespoons olive oil
- Fresh parsley, chopped
- 500g clams, cleaned
- 4 cloves garlic, minced
- Salt and pepper to taste
- 120ml white wine
- Red pepper flakes to taste

Preparation Instructions:
1. Preheat the air fryer to 375°F in Roast mode.
2. Cook linguine according to package instructions; drain and set aside.
3. In a pan, heat olive oil, add minced garlic, and sauté until fragrant.
4. Add cleaned clams, white wine, and red pepper flakes. Roast in the air fryer for 10-12 minutes until the clams open.

5. Toss the cooked linguine with the clam mixture.

6. Season with salt, pepper, and garnish with fresh parsley.

7. Serve immediately for a delightful linguine in white wine sauce.

Mediterranean Baked Cod

Prep Time: 15 minutes / Cook Time: 20 minutes / Servings: 4 / Mode: Roast

Ingredients:

- 4 cod fillets
- 100g Kalamata olives, sliced
- 2 cloves garlic, minced • 30ml olive oil
- 5g dried oregano
- 200g cherry tomatoes, halved
- 50g red onion, finely sliced
- 15ml lemon juice
- Salt and pepper to taste

Preparation Instructions:

1. Preheat the Tower Dual Basket Air Fryer to 400°F in Roast mode.

2. In a bowl, mix together cherry tomatoes, Kalamata olives, red onion, minced garlic, olive oil, lemon juice, dried oregano, salt, and pepper.

3. Place the cod fillets on a baking sheet lined with parchment paper.

4. Spoon the tomato and olive mixture over the cod fillets.

5. Roast for about 20 minutes until the cod is cooked through and flakes easily with a fork.

6. Serve the Mediterranean Baked Cod with your favorite side dishes.

Cajun Blackened Red Snapper

Prep Time: 10 minutes / Cook Time: 10 minutes / Servings: 4 / Mode: Air Fry

Ingredients:

- 4 red snapper fillets
- 10g paprika
- Salt to taste
- 20g Cajun seasoning
- 5g garlic powder
- 30ml olive oil
- 5g onion powder

Preparation Instructions:

1. Preheat the Tower Dual Basket Air Fryer to 375°F in Air Fry mode.

2. In a small bowl, mix Cajun seasoning, olive oil, paprika, garlic powder, onion powder, and salt.

3. Rub the Cajun mixture over both sides of the red snapper fillets.

4. Place the fillets in the air fryer basket.

5. Air fry for about 10 minutes until the fish is blackened and cooked through.

6. Serve the Cajun Blackened Red Snapper with a squeeze of fresh lemon.

Sides and Appetizers

Spinach and Artichoke Dip

Prep Time: 10 minutes / Cook Time: 20 minutes / Servings: 6 / Mode: Bake

Ingredients:

- 200g frozen chopped spinach, thawed and drained
- 200g artichoke hearts, drained and chopped
- 150g cream cheese, softened
- 100g mayonnaise
- 100g sour cream
- 125g shredded mozzarella
- 50g grated Parmesan
- 2 cloves garlic, minced
- Salt and pepper to taste

Preparation Instructions:

1. Preheat the Tower Dual Basket Air Fryer to 375°F in Bake mode.
2. In a large bowl, mix together chopped spinach, chopped artichoke hearts, cream cheese, mayonnaise, sour cream, shredded mozzarella, grated Parmesan, minced garlic, salt, and pepper.
3. Transfer the mixture to a baking dish.
4. Bake for about 20 minutes until the dip is hot and bubbly.
5. Serve the Spinach and Artichoke Dip with tortilla chips or sliced baguette.

Bruschetta with Tomato and Basil

Prep Time: 10 minutes / Cook Time: 5 minutes / Servings: 4 / Mode: Roast

Ingredients:

- 4 large tomatoes, diced
- 15g fresh basil, chopped
- 2 cloves garlic, minced
- 30ml balsamic vinegar
- 30ml olive oil
- Salt and pepper to taste
- Baguette slices for serving

Preparation Instructions:

1. Preheat the Tower Dual Basket Air Fryer to 400°F in Roast mode.
2. In a bowl, combine diced tomatoes, chopped fresh basil, minced garlic, balsamic vinegar, olive oil, salt, and pepper.
3. Arrange baguette slices on the air fryer basket.
4. Roast for about 5 minutes until the bread is toasted.
5. Spoon the tomato and basil mixture over the toasted baguette slices.
6. Serve the Bruschetta with Tomato and Basil as a delightful appetizer.

Deviled Eggs

Prep Time: 15 minutes / Cook Time: Not applicable / Servings: 12 / Mode: Not applicable

Ingredients:

- 6 hard-boiled eggs, peeled and halved
- 60g mayonnaise
- 10g Dijon mustard
- 1 teaspoon white vinegar
- Salt and pepper to taste
- Paprika for garnish

Preparation Instructions:

1. In a bowl, scoop out the egg yolks and mash them with mayonnaise, Dijon mustard, white vinegar, salt, and pepper.
2. Spoon or pipe the yolk mixture back into the egg white halves.
3. Sprinkle paprika over the deviled eggs for garnish.
4. Serve the Deviled Eggs as a classic and delicious appetizer.

Loaded Nachos

Prep Time: 10 minutes / Cook Time: 5 minutes / Servings: 4 / Mode: Air Fry

Ingredients:

- 200g tortilla chips
- 100g shredded cheddar cheese
- 240g black beans, canned and drained
- 240g diced tomatoes
- 120g sliced jalapeños
- 120g sliced black olives
- 60g chopped green onions
- 60g sour cream
- 60g guacamole
- 60g salsa

Preparation Instructions:

1. Preheat the air fryer to 375°F in Air Fry mode.
2. Arrange tortilla chips in a single layer in the air fryer basket.
3. Sprinkle shredded cheddar cheese evenly over the chips..
4. Air fry for 5 minutes or until the cheese is melted and bubbly.
5. Remove from the air fryer and top with black beans, diced tomatoes, jalapeños, black olives, green onions, sour cream, guacamole, and salsa.
6. Serve immediately, and enjoy these delicious loaded nachos.

Stuffed Mushrooms with Cream Cheese

Prep Time: 15 minutes / Cook Time: 12 minutes / Servings: Not specified / Mode: Air Fry

Ingredients:

- 200g button mushrooms, stems removed
- 100g cream cheese
- 2 tablespoons breadcrumbs
- 1 clove garlic, minced
- 1 tablespoon fresh parsley, chopped
- Salt and pepper to taste
- Olive oil spray

Preparation Instructions:

1. In a bowl, mix cream cheese, breadcrumbs, minced garlic, chopped parsley, salt, and pepper.
2. Spoon the cream cheese mixture into the mushroom caps.
3. Preheat the air fryer to 375°F in Air Fry mode.
4. Lightly spray mushrooms with olive oil.
5. Air fry for 12 minutes until the mushrooms are tender and the filling is golden.

Pigs in a Blanket

Prep Time: 10 minutes / Cook Time: 8 minutes / Servings: Not specified / Mode: Air Fry

Ingredients:

- 8 cocktail sausages
- 1 sheet puff pastry, thawed
- Mustard for dipping (optional)

Preparation Instructions:

1. Preheat the air fryer to 375°F in Air Fry mode.
2. Cut the puff pastry into strips and wrap each cocktail sausage.
3. Air fry for 8 minutes until the pastry is golden and cooked through.
4. Serve with mustard for dipping if desired.

Avocado Egg Rolls

Prep Time: 20 minutes / Cook Time: 10 minutes / Servings: 4 / Mode: Air Fry

Ingredients:

- 2 ripe avocados, peeled, pitted, and sliced (about 300g)
- 60g sun-dried tomatoes, chopped
- 40g red onion, finely diced
- 2 tablespoons fresh cilantro, chopped
- Juice of 1 lime
- Salt and pepper to taste

- 8 egg roll wrappers
- Water (for sealing wrappers)
- Cooking spray

Preparation Instructions:
1. In a bowl, combine sliced avocados, sun-dried tomatoes, red onion, cilantro, lime juice, salt, and pepper. Gently mix.
2. Place an egg roll wrapper on a clean surface with one corner pointing toward you. Spoon a portion of the avocado mixture onto the center of the wrapper.
3. Fold the bottom corner over the filling, then fold in the sides, and roll it up tightly, sealing the edges with water.
4. Repeat for remaining wrappers and filling.
5. Preheat the air fryer to 375°F in Air Fry mode.
6. Lightly coat the egg rolls with cooking spray.
7. Air fry for about 10 minutes, turning halfway, until golden and crispy.
8. Serve the avocado egg rolls with your favorite dipping sauce.
9. Enjoy this delicious appetizer with a creamy avocado filling and a crispy exterior.

Bacon-Wrapped Jalapeño Poppers

Prep Time: 20 minutes / Cook Time: 15 minutes / Servings: 4 / Mode: Air Fry

Ingredients:
- 8 large jalapeño peppers
- 200g cream cheese, softened
- 100g shredded cheddar cheese
- 8 slices bacon, cut in half
- Toothpicks for securing

Preparation Instructions:
1. Preheat the air fryer to 375°F in Air Fry mode.
2. Cut jalapeños in half lengthwise, remove seeds, and set aside.
3. In a bowl, mix softened cream cheese and shredded cheddar cheese until well combined.
4. Fill each jalapeño half with the cheese mixture.
5. Wrap each stuffed jalapeño with a half-slice of bacon and secure with toothpicks.
6. Arrange the bacon-wrapped jalapeños in the air fryer basket.
7. Air fry for 15 minutes or until the bacon is crispy.
8. Remove toothpicks before serving.
9. Enjoy these delicious and spicy bacon-wrapped jalapeño poppers.

Baked Brie with Cranberry Sauce

Prep Time: 15 minutes / Cook Time: 15 minutes / Servings: 6 / Mode: Bake

Ingredients:
- 1 wheel of Brie cheese (about 200g)
- 120ml cranberry sauce
- 2 tablespoons chopped pecans
- 1 tablespoon honey
- Fresh rosemary sprigs for garnish

Preparation Instructions:
1. Preheat the oven to 375°F in Bake mode.
2. Place the Brie wheel on a baking sheet lined with parchment paper.
3. Score the top rind of the Brie with a knife to allow for easier spreading after baking.
4. Spread cranberry sauce over the scored Brie.
5. Sprinkle chopped pecans on top and drizzle honey over the cranberry layer.
6. Bake for about 15 minutes or until the Brie is soft and gooey.
7. Remove from the oven and let it cool slightly.
8. Garnish with fresh rosemary sprigs.
9. Serve the baked Brie with crackers or sliced baguette.

10. Indulge in this delightful appetizer with a perfect balance of creamy Brie, sweet cranberry, and crunchy pecans.

Mozzarella Sticks

Prep Time: 10 minutes / Cook Time: 8 minutes / Servings: 4 / Mode: Air Fry

Ingredients:

- 200g mozzarella cheese sticks
- 100g breadcrumbs
- 2 eggs, beaten
- 30ml olive oil
- Marinara sauce for dipping

Preparation Instructions:

1. Preheat the air fryer to 375°F in Air Fry mode.
2. Cut the mozzarella sticks in half.
3. Dip each mozzarella stick into beaten eggs, then coat with breadcrumbs.
4. Place the coated mozzarella sticks in the air fryer basket.
5. Drizzle olive oil over the sticks.
6. Air fry for about 8 minutes until golden and crispy.
7. Serve the mozzarella sticks with marinara sauce for a delicious snack or appetizer.

Buffalo Chicken Wings

Prep Time: 10 minutes / Cook Time: 25 minutes / Servings: 6 / Mode: Air Fry

Ingredients:

- 1 kg chicken wings
- 60g unsalted butter, melted
- 120ml hot sauce
- 1 teaspoon garlic powder
- 1 teaspoon onion powder
- Salt and pepper to taste
- Celery sticks and blue cheese dressing for serving

Preparation Instructions:

1. Preheat the air fryer to 400°F in Air Fry mode.
2. Pat the chicken wings dry with paper towels.
3. In a bowl, mix melted butter, hot sauce, garlic powder, onion powder, salt, and pepper.
4. Toss the chicken wings in the sauce mixture until well coated.
5. Place the wings in a single layer in the air fryer basket.
6. Air fry for 25 minutes, flipping halfway through, until the wings are crispy and golden.
7. Serve the Buffalo Chicken Wings with celery sticks and blue cheese dressing on the side.
8. Enjoy this classic and flavourful appetizer with a spicy kick.

Crab Rangoon

Prep Time: 20 minutes / Cook Time: 10 minutes / Servings: 4 / Mode: Air Fry

Ingredients:

- 150g cream cheese, softened
- 120g canned crab meat, drained and flaked
- 2 green onions, finely chopped
- 1 garlic clove, minced
- 1 teaspoon Worcestershire sauce
- Salt and pepper to taste
- 16 wonton wrappers
- Cooking spray

Preparation Instructions:

1. In a bowl, combine softened cream cheese, crab meat, green onions, minced garlic, Worcestershire sauce, salt, and pepper.
2. Lay out the wonton wrappers on a clean surface.
3. Place a spoonful of the cream cheese and crab mixture in the center of each wrapper.
4. Moisten the edges of the wrappers with water and fold them over to create triangles, pressing the

edges to seal.

5. Preheat the air fryer to 375°F in Air Fry mode.
6. Spray the crab Rangoon with cooking spray and place them in the air fryer basket in a single layer.
7. Air fry for about 8-10 minutes until they are golden brown and crispy.
8. Serve the Crab Rangoon with your favorite dipping sauce.

Asparagus Wrapped in Prosciutto

Prep Time: 10 minutes / Cook Time: 15 minutes / Servings: 4 / Mode: Air Fry

Ingredients:

- 16 asparagus spears, trimmed
- 8 slices prosciutto
- Olive oil for brushing
- Salt and pepper to taste
- Lemon wedges for serving (optional)

Preparation Instructions:

1. Preheat the air fryer to 375°F in Air Fry mode.
2. Bundle 4 asparagus spears together and wrap each bundle with 2 slices of prosciutto, securing the ends.
3. Repeat the process for the remaining asparagus and prosciutto.
4. Lightly brush the wrapped asparagus with olive oil.
5. Sprinkle with salt and pepper to taste.
6. Place the asparagus bundles in the air fryer basket.
7. Air fry for about 12-15 minutes, turning halfway through, or until the prosciutto is crispy and the asparagus is tender.
8. Remove from the air fryer and squeeze fresh lemon juice over the top if desired.
9. Serve these delightful Asparagus Wrapped in Prosciutto as an elegant appetizer or side dish. Enjoy!

Bacon-Wrapped Dates with Goat Cheese

Prep Time: 20 minutes / Cook Time: 15 minutes / Servings: 4 / Mode: Air Fry

Ingredients:

- 12 Medjool dates, pitted
- 60g goat cheese
- 6 slices bacon, cut in half
- Toothpicks for securing

Preparation Instructions:

1. Preheat the air fryer to 375°F in Air Fry mode.
2. Stuff each pitted date with goat cheese.
3. Wrap each stuffed date with a half-slice of bacon, securing with a toothpick.
4. Place the bacon-wrapped dates in the air fryer basket.
5. Air fry for approximately 12-15 minutes until the bacon is crispy.
6. Remove toothpicks before serving.
7. Serve these sweet and savory Bacon-Wrapped Dates with Goat Cheese for an irresistible appetizer.
8. Enjoy the delightful combination of flavours in each bite.

Roasted Garlic and Rosemary Potato Wedges

Prep Time: 15 minutes / Cook Time: 30 minutes / Servings: 4 / Mode: Roast

Ingredients:

- 4 large potatoes, cut into wedges
- 3 tablespoons olive oil
- 4 cloves garlic, minced
- 1 tablespoon fresh rosemary, chopped
- Salt and black pepper to taste

Preparation Instructions:

1. Preheat the oven to 425°F in Roast mode.
2. In a large bowl, toss the potato wedges with olive oil, minced garlic, and chopped rosemary until

evenly coated.

3. Spread the wedges in a single layer on a baking sheet.
4. Season with salt and black pepper to taste.
5. Roast in the preheated oven for about 30 minutes or until the potatoes are golden brown and crispy.
6. Remove from the oven and serve the Roasted Garlic and Rosemary Potato Wedges as a flavourful side dish.
7. Enjoy the delicious combination of roasted garlic and rosemary with perfectly cooked potato wedges!

Grilled Portobello Mushrooms with Balsamic Glaze

Prep Time: 10 minutes / Cook Time: 15 minutes / Servings: 2 / Mode: Roast

Ingredients:
- 4 large portobello mushrooms, stems removed
- 2 tablespoons olive oil
- Salt and black pepper to taste
- 3 tablespoons balsamic glaze
- 2 cloves garlic, minced
- Fresh parsley for garnish (optional)

Preparation Instructions:
1. Preheat the Air Fryer to medium-high heat.
2. In a small bowl, whisk together balsamic glaze, olive oil, minced garlic, salt, and black pepper.
3. Brush the mushroom caps with the prepared balsamic mixture.
4. Place the mushrooms on the preheated Air Fryer and cook for about 5-7 minutes per side or until tender.
5. Brush with additional balsamic glaze during grilling if desired.
6. Remove from the Air Fryer and garnish with fresh parsley if using.
7. Serve the Grilled Portobello Mushrooms with Balsamic Glaze as a delightful vegetarian option.

Spanakopita (Spinach and Feta Triangles)

Prep Time: 30 minutes / Cook Time: 20 minutes / Servings: 6 / Mode: Bake

Ingredients:
- 200g fresh spinach, chopped
- 2 cloves garlic, minced
- 1 package phyllo pastry sheets (12 sheets)
- 100g feta cheese, crumbled
- 2 tablespoons olive oil
- 1 small onion, finely chopped
- Salt and black pepper to taste
- Cooking spray or extra olive oil for brushing

Preparation Instructions:
1. Preheat the oven to 375°F in Bake mode.
2. In a pan, sauté chopped onion and minced garlic in olive oil until softened.
3. Add chopped spinach to the pan and cook until wilted. Season with salt and black pepper. Allow the mixture to cool.
4. In a large bowl, combine the cooled spinach mixture with crumbled feta cheese.
5. Lay out one sheet of phyllo pastry, brush it lightly with olive oil or use cooking spray, and place another sheet on top. Repeat until you have a stack of 3 sheets.
6. Spoon a portion of the spinach and feta mixture onto the phyllo stack.
7. Fold the phyllo sheets over the filling to create a triangle shape. Repeat with the remaining sheets and filling.
8. Place the triangles on a baking sheet, seam side down.
9. Bake in the preheated oven for about 20 minutes or until golden brown and crispy.
10. Serve the Spanakopita triangles warm as a delicious appetizer or snack.
11. Enjoy the classic combination of spinach and feta in a flaky phyllo pastry!

Cranberry and Brie Phyllo Cups

Prep Time: 15 minutes / Cook Time: 10 minutes / Servings: 6 / Mode: Bake

Ingredients:
- 240g cranberry sauce
- 2 tablespoons melted butter
- Fresh rosemary for garnish
- 150g Brie cheese, cut into small pieces
- 1 package (about 12 sheets) phyllo pastry

Preparation Instructions:
1. Preheat the air fryer to 375°F in Bake mode.
2. Cut the phyllo sheets into squares or rectangles.
3. Layer 2-3 pieces of phyllo, brushing each layer with melted butter.
4. Place a small spoonful of cranberry sauce and a piece of Brie in the center of each phyllo square.
5. Fold the phyllo around the filling to form small cups.
6. Brush the tops with more melted butter.
7. Air fry for about 8-10 minutes until the phyllo is golden and crispy.
8. Garnish with fresh rosemary.
9. Serve these delightful Cranberry and Brie Phyllo Cups as a festive appetizer.

Baked Buffalo Cauliflower Bites

Prep Time: 15 minutes / Cook Time: 20 minutes / Servings: 4 / Mode: Bake

Ingredients:
- 1 head cauliflower, cut into florets (about 600g)
- 120ml buffalo sauce
- 60g melted butter
- 1 teaspoon garlic powder
- 1 teaspoon onion powder
- Salt and pepper to taste
- Fresh parsley for garnish

Preparation Instructions:
1. Preheat the air fryer to 375°F in Bake mode.
2. In a bowl, whisk together buffalo sauce, melted butter, garlic powder, onion powder, salt, and pepper.
3. Toss cauliflower florets in the buffalo sauce mixture until well coated.
4. Place the coated cauliflower in the air fryer basket in a single layer.
5. Air fry for about 15-20 minutes, shaking the basket halfway through, until the cauliflower is crispy.
6. Garnish with fresh parsley.
7. Serve these Baked Buffalo Cauliflower Bites as a flavourful and healthier alternative to traditional buffalo wings.

Artichoke and Spinach Stuffed Mini Peppers

Prep Time: 20 minutes / Cook Time: 15 minutes / Servings: 4 / Mode: Bake

Ingredients:
- 200g mini sweet peppers, halved and seeds removed
- 150g frozen chopped spinach, thawed and drained
- 100g artichoke hearts, chopped
- 100g cream cheese, softened
- 50g shredded mozzarella cheese
- 2 cloves garlic, minced
- 1 tablespoon olive oil
- Salt and pepper to taste
- Fresh basil for garnish

Preparation Instructions:
1. Preheat the air fryer to 375°F in Bake mode.
2. In a bowl, combine thawed and drained chopped spinach, chopped artichoke hearts, cream cheese, shredded mozzarella, minced garlic, olive oil, salt, and pepper.
3. Stuff each mini pepper half with the artichoke and spinach mixture.
4. Place the stuffed peppers in the air fryer basket in a single layer.
5. Air fry for about 12-15 minutes until the peppers are tender and the filling is bubbly.
6. Garnish with fresh basil.
7. Serve these Artichoke and Spinach Stuffed Mini Peppers as a delightful appetizer or snack.

Vegan and Veggies

Vegan Buffalo Cauliflower Wings

Prep Time: 15 minutes / Cook Time: 20 minutes / Servings: 4 / Mode: Air Fry

Ingredients:
- 1 head cauliflower, cut into florets
- 120ml plant-based milk (120ml)
- 1 teaspoon onion powder
- Salt and pepper to taste
- Vegan ranch dressing for dipping
- 60g all-purpose flour (60g)
- 1 teaspoon garlic powder
- 1/2 teaspoon smoked paprika
- 120ml buffalo sauce

Preparation Instructions:
1. In a bowl, whisk together all-purpose flour, plant-based milk, garlic powder, onion powder, smoked paprika, salt, and pepper to create a batter.
2. Dip each cauliflower floret into the batter, ensuring they are well-coated.
3. Place the battered cauliflower in the air fryer basket, leaving space between each piece.
4. Air fry at 375°F for 15-20 minutes or until the cauliflower is golden and crisp.
5. In a separate bowl, toss the air-fried cauliflower in buffalo sauce until evenly coated.
6. Serve the Vegan Buffalo Cauliflower Wings with vegan ranch dressing for dipping.

Vegan Buffalo Cauliflower Bites

Prep Time: 15 minutes / Cook Time: 20 minutes / Servings: 4 / Mode: Air Fry

Ingredients:
- 1 head cauliflower, cut into florets
- 120ml plant-based milk
- 1 teaspoon onion powder
- Salt and pepper to taste • 120ml buffalo sauce
- 60g all-purpose flour
- 1 teaspoon garlic powder
- 1/2 teaspoon smoked paprika
- Vegan ranch dressing for dipping

Preparation Instructions:
1. In a bowl, whisk together 60g all-purpose flour, 120ml plant-based milk, garlic powder, onion powder, smoked paprika, salt, and pepper to create a batter.
2. Dip each cauliflower floret into the batter, ensuring they are well-coated.
3. Place the battered cauliflower in the air fryer basket, leaving space between each piece.
4. Air fry at 375°F for 15-20 minutes or until the cauliflower is golden and crisp.
5. In a separate bowl, toss the air-fried cauliflower in 120ml buffalo sauce until evenly coated.
6. Serve the Vegan Buffalo Cauliflower Bites with vegan ranch dressing for dipping.

Roasted Chickpeas with Herbs

Prep Time: 10 minutes / Cook Time: 15 minutes / Servings: 4 / Mode: Air Fry

Ingredients:
- 2 cans (400g each) chickpeas, drained and rinsed
- 1 teaspoon garlic powder
- 1 teaspoon smoked paprika
- 2 tablespoons olive oil
- 1 teaspoon dried rosemary
- Salt and pepper to taste

Preparation Instructions:
1. In a bowl, toss chickpeas with olive oil, garlic powder, dried rosemary, smoked paprika, salt, and

pepper.

2. Spread the chickpeas in a single layer in the air fryer basket.
3. Air fry at 375°F for 15 minutes, shaking the basket halfway through.
4. Once chickpeas are crispy and golden, remove from the air fryer and let them cool slightly.
5. Serve the Roasted Chickpeas with Herbs as a crunchy and flavourful snack.

Roasted Vegetable Skewers

Prep Time: 15 minutes / Cook Time: 20 minutes / Servings: 4 / Mode: Air Fry

Ingredients:
- Assorted vegetables (bell peppers, cherry tomatoes, zucchini, mushrooms), cut into chunks
- 2 tablespoons olive oil
- 1 teaspoon garlic powder
- 1 teaspoon dried oregano
- Salt and pepper to taste

Preparation Instructions:
1. In a bowl, toss vegetable chunks with olive oil, dried oregano, garlic powder, salt, and pepper.
2. Thread the vegetables onto skewers, alternating varieties.
3. Place the vegetable skewers in the air fryer basket.
4. Air fry at 375°F for 20 minutes, turning the skewers halfway through.
5. Once the vegetables are tender and slightly charred, remove from the air fryer.
6. Serve the Roasted Vegetable Skewers as a delightful and colorful side dish.

Roasted Root Vegetable Medley

Prep Time: 15 minutes / Cook Time: 35 minutes / Servings: 4 / Mode: Roast

Ingredients:
- 2 parsnips, peeled and diced
- 1 red onion, sliced
- 1 teaspoon rosemary
- 2 carrots, peeled and diced
- 2 tablespoons olive oil
- Salt and pepper to taste
- 2 turnips, peeled and diced
- 1 teaspoon thyme

Preparation Instructions:
1. Preheat the Air Fryer to 400°F in Roast mode.
2. In a roasting pan, toss diced parsnips, carrots, turnips, and sliced red onion
3. In a roasting pan, toss diced parsnips, carrots, turnips, and sliced red onion with olive oil, thyme, rosemary, salt, and pepper.
4. Spread the vegetables in a single layer.
5. Roast in the Air Fryer at 400°F for 35 minutes or until the vegetables are tender and caramelised.
6. Stir the vegetables halfway through the roasting time for even cooking.
7. Once roasted, remove from the Air Fryer and serve this flavourful Roasted Root Vegetable Medley as a delightful side dish.

Vegan Shepherd's Pie Stuffed Bell Peppers

Prep Time: 20 minutes / Cook Time: 30 minutes / Servings: 4 / Mode: Air Fry

Ingredients:
- 4 large bell peppers, halved and seeds removed
- 1 onion, finely chopped
- 2 celery stalks, diced
- 400g canned diced tomatoes
- 1 teaspoon rosemary
- Mashed sweet potatoes for topping
- 200g lentils, cooked
- 2 carrots, diced
- 2 cloves garlic, minced
- 1 teaspoon thyme
- Salt and pepper to taste

Preparation Instructions:

1. Preheat the air fryer to 375°F in Air Fry mode.
2. In a pan, sauté onions, carrots, celery, and garlic until softened.
3. Add cooked lentils, diced tomatoes, thyme, rosemary, salt, and pepper. Cook until well combined.
4. Fill each bell pepper half with the lentil mixture.
5. Place the stuffed peppers in the air fryer basket.
6. Air fry for 25-30 minutes until the peppers are tender.
7. Top each stuffed pepper with mashed sweet potatoes before serving.

Baked Beetroot and Lentil Burgers

Prep Time: 15 minutes / Cook Time: 25 minutes / Servings: 4 / Mode: Bake

Ingredients:

- 250g cooked beetroots, grated
- 200g cooked green lentils
- 1 onion, finely chopped
- 2 cloves garlic, minced
- 50g breadcrumbs
- 1 teaspoon cumin
- 1 teaspoon smoked paprika
- Salt and pepper to taste
- Burger buns and toppings of choice

Preparation Instructions:

1. Preheat the Air Fryer to 375°F in Bake mode.
2. In a bowl, combine grated beetroots, cooked lentils, chopped onion, minced garlic, breadcrumbs, cumin, smoked paprika, salt, and pepper.
3. Form the mixture into burger patties and place them on a baking sheet.
4. Bake for 20-25 minutes until the burgers are firm and golden.
5. Serve the Beetroot and Lentil Burgers in burger buns with your favorite toppings.

Vegan Mushroom and Leek Wellington

Prep Time: 25 minutes / Cook Time: 35 minutes / Servings: 4 / Mode: Roast

Ingredients:

- 1 sheet vegan puff pastry
- 200g mushrooms, finely chopped
- 2 leeks, sliced
- 2 cloves garlic, minced
- 1 tablespoon olive oil
- 1 teaspoon thyme
- Salt and pepper to taste
- Vegan puff pastry for wrapping

Preparation Instructions:

1. Preheat the Air Fryer to 400°F in Roast mode.
2. In a pan, sauté mushrooms, leeks, and garlic in olive oil until softened.
3. Season with thyme, salt, and pepper.
4. Roll out the vegan puff pastry sheet and place the mushroom and leek mixture on it.
5. Fold the pastry over the filling, sealing the edges.
6. Roast for 25-30 minutes until the pastry is golden and crisp.
7. Slice and serve this Vegan Mushroom and Leek Wellington as a savoury centrepiece.

Roasted Brussels Sprouts with Balsamic Glaze

Prep Time: 15 minutes / Cook Time: 25 minutes / Servings: 4 / Mode: Air Fry

Ingredients:

- 500g Brussels sprouts, trimmed and halved
- 2 tablespoons olive oil
- 2 tablespoons balsamic glaze
- Salt and pepper to taste

Preparation Instructions:

1. Preheat the air fryer to 375°F in Air Fry mode.

2. Toss Brussels sprouts with olive oil, salt, and pepper.
3. Place the Brussels sprouts in the air fryer basket.
4. Air fry for 20-25 minutes until they are crispy and golden.
5. Drizzle balsamic glaze over the roasted Brussels sprouts before serving.

Vegan BBQ Cauliflower Bites

Prep Time: 15 minutes / Cook Time: 20 minutes / Servings: 4 / Mode: Air Fry

Ingredients:
- 1 small head cauliflower, cut into florets
- 120ml almond milk
- 1 teaspoon smoked paprika
- 1/2 teaspoon onion powder
- 120ml vegan barbecue sauce
- 100g chickpea flour
- 1 teaspoon garlic powder
- Salt and pepper to taste

Preparation Instructions:
1. Preheat the air fryer to 375°F in Air Fry mode.
2. In a bowl, whisk together chickpea flour, almond milk, smoked paprika, garlic powder, onion powder, salt, and pepper to create a batter.
3. Dip cauliflower florets into the batter, ensuring they are well coated.
4. Arrange the coated cauliflower in the air fryer basket.
5. Air fry for 15-20 minutes, pausing to shake the basket halfway through.
6. Toss the cooked cauliflower bites in vegan barbecue sauce before serving.
7. Enjoy these flavourful and crispy vegan BBQ cauliflower bites as a tasty snack or appetizer.

Vegan Spinach and Artichoke Stuffed Mushrooms

Prep Time: 15 minutes / Cook Time: 20 minutes / Servings: 4 / Mode: Air Fry

Ingredients:
- 16 large mushrooms, cleaned and stems removed
- 150g frozen spinach, thawed and squeezed dry
- 1 clove garlic, minced
- 30g nutritional yeast
- Olive oil for brushing
- 100g artichoke hearts, finely chopped
- 50g vegan cream cheese
- Salt and pepper to taste

Preparation Instructions:
1. Preheat the air fryer to 375°F in Air Fry mode.
2. In a bowl, combine spinach, artichoke hearts, garlic, vegan cream cheese, nutritional yeast, salt, and pepper.
3. Stuff each mushroom cap with the spinach and artichoke mixture.
4. Lightly brush the stuffed mushrooms with olive oil.
5. Air fry for 15-20 minutes until the mushrooms are tender and the filling is golden.
6. Serve these vegan stuffed mushrooms as a delightful appetizer or side dish.

Vegan Spinach and Mushroom Stuffed Portobello Mushrooms

Prep Time: 20 minutes / Cook Time: 25 minutes / Servings: 4 / Mode: Bake

Ingredients:
- 4 large portobello mushrooms
- 1 onion, minced
- 50g vegan breadcrumbs
- 200g spinach, chopped
- 2 cloves garlic, minced
- Salt and pepper to taste
- 150g mushrooms, finely diced
- 2 tablespoons olive oil

Preparation Instructions:
1. Preheat the Air Fryer to 375°F in Bake mode.

2. Remove the stems from portobello mushrooms and clean the caps.
3. In a pan, sauté onion, garlic, spinach, and mushrooms in olive oil until softened.
4. Season with salt and pepper.
5. Fill each portobello cap with the sautéed mixture, top with breadcrumbs.
6. Bake for 20-25 minutes until mushrooms are tender and breadcrumbs are golden.
7. Serve these flavourful stuffed mushrooms as a satisfying appetizer or main course.

Roasted Root Vegetable Salad with Maple-Dijon Dressing

Prep Time: 15 minutes / Roast Time: 30 minutes / Servings: 4 / Mode: Roast

Ingredients:
- 2 parsnips, peeled and diced
- 1 sweet potato, peeled and diced
- 2 tablespoons olive oil
- 1 tablespoon Dijon mustard
- 2 carrots, peeled and diced
- 1 red onion, sliced
- 2 tablespoons maple syrup
- Salt and pepper to taste

Preparation Instructions:
1. Preheat the Air Fryer to 400°F in Roast mode.
2. Toss parsnips, carrots, sweet potato, and red onion in olive oil.
3. Roast for 30 minutes until vegetables are tender and caramelised.
4. In a small bowl, whisk together maple syrup, Dijon mustard, salt, and pepper.
5. Drizzle the dressing over the roasted vegetables.
6. Toss gently and serve this delightful Roasted Root Vegetable Salad as a side dish or light meal.

Vegan Sweet Potato Falafel

Prep Time: 15 minutes / Cook Time: 20 minutes / Servings: 4 / Mode: Air Fry

Ingredients:
- 400g sweet potatoes, cooked and mashed
- 1 small red onion, finely chopped
- 1 teaspoon ground cumin
- Handful of fresh parsley, chopped
- Salt and pepper to taste
- 1 can (400g) chickpeas, drained
- 2 cloves garlic, minced
- 1 teaspoon ground coriander
- 2 tablespoons chickpea flour

Preparation Instructions:
1. Preheat the air fryer to 375°F in Air Fry mode.
2. In a food processor, combine sweet potatoes, chickpeas, red onion, garlic, cumin, coriander, parsley, chickpea flour, salt, and pepper. Pulse until well mixed.
3. Form the mixture into small falafel balls.
4. Arrange the falafel in the air fryer basket.
5. Air fry for 15-20 minutes until golden brown and crispy.
6. Serve these vegan sweet potato falafel with your favorite dipping sauce or in a wrap.
7. Enjoy a delightful and nutritious plant-based meal.

Vegan Mediterranean Quinoa Salad

Prep Time: 15 minutes / Cook Time: 20 minutes / Servings: 4 / Mode: Air Fry

Ingredients:
- 180g quinoa, cooked
- 1 cucumber, diced
- 25g red onion, finely chopped
- 150g cherry tomatoes, halved
- 50g Kalamata olives, sliced
- 2 tablespoons fresh parsley, chopped

- 45ml olive oil
- Salt and pepper to taste
- Juice of 1 lemon

Preparation Instructions:
- 1. Preheat the air fryer to 375°F in Air Fry mode.
2. In a bowl, combine cooked quinoa, cherry tomatoes, cucumber, olives, red onion, parsley, olive oil, lemon juice, salt, and pepper.
3. Mix well to ensure all ingredients are evenly coated.
4. Air fry for 15-20 minutes, shaking the basket halfway through.
5. Serve this refreshing Mediterranean quinoa salad as a light and satisfying dish.

Vegan Buffalo Cauliflower Tacos

Prep Time: 15 minutes / Cook Time: 20 minutes / Servings: 4 / Mode: Air Fry

Ingredients:
- 1 small head cauliflower, cut into florets
- 120ml almond milk
- 1/2 teaspoon smoked paprika
- 1 teaspoon garlic powder
- 120ml vegan buffalo sauce
- 100g chickpea flour
- 1 teaspoon onion powder
- Corn tortillas
- Shredded lettuce, diced tomatoes, and avocado for toppings

Preparation Instructions:
1. Preheat the air fryer to 375°F in Air Fry mode.
2. In a bowl, whisk together chickpea flour, almond milk, garlic powder, onion powder, and smoked paprika to create a batter.
3. Dip cauliflower florets into the batter, ensuring they are well coated.
4. Arrange the coated cauliflower in the air fryer basket.
5. Air fry for 15-20 minutes, pausing to shake the basket halfway through.
6. Toss the cooked cauliflower in vegan buffalo sauce.
7. Assemble tacos with buffalo cauliflower, shredded lettuce, diced tomatoes, and avocado.
8. Enjoy these flavourful and spicy vegan buffalo cauliflower tacos.

Vegan Mediterranean Stuffed Bell Peppers

Prep Time: 15 minutes / Cook Time: 25 minutes / Servings: 4 / Mode: Air Fry

Ingredients:
- 4 bell peppers, halved and seeds removed
- 150g cherry tomatoes, halved
- 50g Kalamata olives, sliced
- 30ml olive oil
- Salt and pepper to taste
- 200g quinoa, cooked
- 100g cucumber, diced
- 25g fresh parsley, chopped
- Juice of 1 lemon

Preparation Instructions:
1. Preheat the air fryer to 375°F in Air Fry mode.
2. In a bowl, combine cooked quinoa, cherry tomatoes, cucumber, olives, parsley, olive oil, lemon juice, salt, and pepper.
3. Stuff each bell pepper half with the quinoa mixture.
4. Air fry for 20-25 minutes until the peppers are tender.
5. Serve these vibrant stuffed peppers as a nutritious and flavourful meal.

Vegan Chickpea Tikka Masala

Prep Time: 15 minutes / Cook Time: 25 minutes / Servings: 4 / Mode: Air Fry

Ingredients:

- 2 cans (800g) chickpeas, drained
- 3 tomatoes, diced
- 1 tablespoon ginger, grated
- 200ml coconut milk
- Salt and pepper to taste
- 1 onion, finely chopped
- 2 cloves garlic, minced
- 2 tablespoons tikka masala spice blend
- Fresh coriander for garnish

Preparation Instructions:

1. Preheat the air fryer to 375°F in Air Fry mode.
2. In a pan, sauté onions, garlic, and ginger until fragrant.
3. Add diced tomatoes, tikka masala spice blend, salt, and pepper. Cook until tomatoes soften.
4. Stir in chickpeas and coconut milk. Simmer until the sauce thickens.
5. Transfer the mixture to the air fryer basket and air fry for 15-20 minutes.
6. Garnish with fresh coriander before serving.

Vegan Lentil and Vegetable Stew

Prep Time: 20 minutes / Cook Time: 25 minutes / Servings: 4 / Mode: Air Fry

Ingredients:

- 200g green lentils, cooked
- 2 celery stalks, chopped
- 1 teaspoon thyme
- 750ml vegetable broth
- 1 onion, chopped
- 3 cloves garlic, minced
- 1 teaspoon rosemary
- Salt and pepper to taste
- 2 carrots, sliced
- 400g canned diced tomatoes
- 1 bay leaf

Preparation Instructions:

1. Preheat the air fryer to 375°F in Air Fry mode.
2. In a pot, sauté onions, carrots, celery, and garlic until softened.
3. Add cooked lentils, diced tomatoes, thyme, rosemary, bay leaf, vegetable broth, salt, and pepper.
4. Transfer the stew mixture to the air fryer basket and air fry for 20-25 minutes.
5. Serve this hearty vegan stew with crusty bread for a satisfying meal.

Vegan Mediterranean Stuffed Zucchini

Prep Time: 15 minutes / Cook Time: 20 minutes / Servings: 4 / Mode: Air Fry

Ingredients:

- 4 medium zucchinis, halved lengthwise
- 150g quinoa, cooked
- 75g cucumber, finely chopped
- 20g fresh mint, chopped
- Salt and pepper to taste
- Juice of 1 lemon
- 100g cherry tomatoes, diced
- 30g black olives, sliced
- 30ml olive oil

Preparation Instructions:

1. Preheat the air fryer to 375°F in Air Fry mode.
2. Scoop out the centre of each zucchini half, leaving a boat-like shape.
3. In a bowl, mix cooked quinoa, cherry tomatoes, cucumber, olives, mint, olive oil, lemon juice, salt, and pepper.
4. Stuff each zucchini half with the quinoa mixture.
5. Air fry for 15-20 minutes until the zucchinis are tender.
6. Serve these Mediterranean stuffed zucchinis for a light and flavourful vegan dish.

Vegan Air Fryer Tofu Nuggets

Prep Time: 15 minutes / Cook Time: 15 minutes / Servings: 4 / Mode: Air Fry

Ingredients:

- 1 block (400g) extra-firm tofu, pressed and cubed
- 1 tablespoon nutritional yeast
- 1 teaspoon smoked paprika
- 60g breadcrumbs (made from whole grain bread)
- 2 tablespoons soy sauce
- 1 teaspoon garlic powder

Preparation Instructions:

1. Preheat the air fryer to 375°F in Air Fry mode.
2. In a bowl, marinate tofu cubes in soy sauce, nutritional yeast, garlic powder, and smoked paprika.
3. Coat each tofu cube in breadcrumbs.
4. Arrange the breaded tofu in the air fryer basket.
5. Air fry for 12-15 minutes until golden and crispy.
6. Serve these flavourful vegan air fryer tofu nuggets with your favorite dipping sauce.

Crispy Zucchini Fries

Prep Time: 10 minutes / Cook Time: 12 minutes / Servings: 4 / Mode: Air Fry

Ingredients:

- 2 medium zucchini, cut into fries
- 1 teaspoon garlic powder
- 1/2 teaspoon paprika
- 60g chickpea flour
- 1/2 teaspoon onion powder
- Salt and pepper to taste

Preparation Instructions:

1. Preheat the air fryer to 375°F in Air Fry mode.
2. In a bowl, combine chickpea flour, garlic powder, onion powder, paprika, salt, and pepper.
3. Toss zucchini fries in the flour mixture until well-coated.
4. Arrange the coated zucchini in the air fryer basket.
5. Air fry for 10-12 minutes until the fries are crispy and golden.
6. Serve these vegan air fryer crispy zucchini fries as a delightful snack or side dish.

Sweet Snacks and Desserts

Chocolate Chip Cookies

Prep Time: 15 minutes / Cook Time: 12 minutes / Servings: 24 cookies / Mode: Bake

Ingredients:
- 200g unsalted butter, softened
- 2 large eggs
- 5g baking soda
- 150g granulated sugar
- 5ml vanilla extract
- 3g salt
- 150g brown sugar
- 375g all-purpose flour
- 200g chocolate chips

Preparation Instructions:
1. Preheat the Air Fryer to 350°F in Bake mode.
2. In a large bowl, cream together softened butter, granulated sugar, and brown sugar until smooth.
3. Beat in the eggs one at a time, then stir in the vanilla extract.
4. In a separate bowl, whisk together all-purpose flour, baking soda, and salt.
5. Gradually add the dry ingredients to the wet ingredients, mixing until well combined.
6. Fold in the chocolate chips.
7. Drop rounded tablespoons of cookie dough onto baking sheets.
8. Bake for 12 minutes or until the edges are golden.
9. Allow the Chocolate Chip Cookies to cool on the baking sheets for a few minutes before transferring to a wire rack.
10. Enjoy these classic cookies with a glass of milk or your favorite beverage.

Brownie Bites

Prep Time: 15 minutes / Cook Time: 20 minutes / Servings: 24 bites / Mode: Bake

Ingredients:
- 150g unsalted butter, melted
- 5ml vanilla extract
- 2g salt
- 200g granulated sugar
- 75g all-purpose flour
- 100g chocolate chips
- 2 large eggs
- 30g cocoa powder

Preparation Instructions:
1. Preheat the Air Fryer to 350°F in Bake mode.
2. In a bowl, combine melted butter, granulated sugar, eggs, and vanilla extract.
3. In a separate bowl, whisk together all-purpose flour, cocoa powder, and salt.
4. Gradually add the dry ingredients to the wet ingredients, mixing until well combined.
5. Fold in the chocolate chips.
6. Spoon the brownie batter into a mini muffin tin.
7. Bake for 20 minutes or until a toothpick comes out with moist crumbs.
8. Allow the Brownie Bites to cool in the tin before transferring to a serving plate.
9. Enjoy these irresistible bite-sized brownies as a sweet treat.

Roasted Garlic Rosemary Nuts

Prep Time: 5 minutes / Roast Time: 15 minutes / Servings: 4 / Mode: Roast

Ingredients:
- 200g mixed nuts (almonds, walnuts, cashews)
- 1 teaspoon garlic powder
- 1 teaspoon dried rosemary
- 2 tablespoons olive oil
- Salt to taste

Preparation Instructions:
1. Preheat the Air Fryer to 350°F.

2. In a bowl, toss mixed nuts with olive oil, garlic powder, dried rosemary, and salt.
3. Spread the seasoned nuts on a baking sheet.
4. Roast in the Air Fryer for 15 minutes or until golden and fragrant.
5. Allow the Roasted Garlic Rosemary Nuts to cool before serving as a flavourful and crunchy snack.

Jam-Filled Doughnuts

Prep Time: 10 minutes / Air Fry Time: 8 minutes / Servings: 6 / Mode: Air Fry

Ingredients:
- 1 sheet ready-rolled puff pastry
- 2 tablespoons melted vegan butter
- 3 tablespoons strawberry jam
- 2 tablespoons granulated sugar

Preparation Instructions:
1. Preheat the air fryer to 375°F.
2. Roll out the puff pastry and cut circles using a cookie cutter.
3. Place a small amount of strawberry jam in the center of half the circles.
4. Top with the remaining circles and seal the edges.
5. Brush each doughnut with melted vegan butter and sprinkle with granulated sugar.
6. Air fry for 8 minutes or until golden and puffed.
7. Allow the Air Fryer Jam-Filled Doughnuts to cool slightly before indulging in this delightful sweet treat.

Banana Bread Muffins

Prep Time: 15 minutes / Cook Time: 18 minutes / Servings: 12 muffins / Mode: Bake

Ingredients:
- 3 ripe bananas, mashed
- 150g granulated sugar
- 5g baking powder
- 50g chopped walnuts (optional)
- 120ml vegetable oil
- 5ml vanilla extract
- 2g baking soda
- 2 large eggs
- 240g all-purpose flour
- 2g salt

Preparation Instructions:
1. Preheat the air fryer to 350°F in Bake mode.
2. In a bowl, whisk together mashed bananas, vegetable oil, eggs, granulated sugar, and vanilla extract.
3. In a separate bowl, combine all-purpose flour, baking powder, baking soda, and salt.
4. Gradually add the dry ingredients to the wet ingredients, mixing until just combined.
5. Fold in chopped walnuts if desired.
6. Spoon the batter into muffin cups, filling each about two-thirds full.
7. Place the muffin cups in the air fryer basket, leaving space between each.
8. Bake for 18 minutes or until a toothpick inserted into the center comes out clean.
9. Allow the Banana Bread Muffins to cool in the muffin tin before transferring to a wire rack.
10. Enjoy these moist and flavourful muffins as a delicious snack or breakfast option.

Raspberry Almond Thumbprint Cookies

Prep Time: 15 minutes / Bake Time: 10 minutes / Servings: 24 cookies / Mode: Bake

Ingredients:
- 150g almond flour
- 60ml coconut oil, melted
- Raspberry jam for filling
- 50g coconut flour
- 5ml almond extract
- 80ml maple syrup
- 1/4 teaspoon salt

Preparation Instructions:
1. Preheat the air fryer to 350°F in Bake mode.
2. In a bowl, combine almond flour, coconut flour, maple syrup, melted coconut oil, almond extract,

and salt.
3. Mix until a dough forms.
4. Roll the dough into small balls and place them on a parchment-lined baking sheet.
5. Use your thumb to make an indentation in each cookie.
6. Fill each indentation with a small spoonful of raspberry jam.
7. Bake for 10 minutes or until the edges are golden.
8. Allow the Raspberry Almond Thumbprint Cookies to cool on the baking sheet before transferring to a serving plate.
9. Enjoy these delightful and nutty cookies with a burst of raspberry sweetness.

Lemon Bars

Prep Time: 15 minutes / Bake Time: 25 minutes / Servings: 16 bars / Mode: Bake

Ingredients:
* For the Crust:
* 180g all-purpose flour
* 75g powdered sugar
* 150g unsalted butter, softened
* For the Lemon Filling:
* 300g granulated sugar
* 4 large eggs
* 120ml lemon juice
* 10g lemon zest
* 30g all-purpose flour
* 1/2 teaspoon baking powder
* Powdered sugar for dusting

Preparation Instructions:
1. Preheat the air fryer to 350°F in Bake mode.
2. In a bowl, combine all-purpose flour, powdered sugar, and softened unsalted butter to create the crust.
3. Press the crust mixture into the bottom of a parchment-lined baking dish.
4. Bake the crust for 15 minutes or until lightly golden.
5. In another bowl, whisk together granulated sugar, eggs, lemon juice, lemon zest, all-purpose flour, and baking powder for the lemon filling.
6. Pour the lemon filling over the baked crust.
7. Bake for an additional 25 minutes or until the edges are set and the center is slightly firm.
8. Allow the Lemon Bars to cool before dusting with powdered sugar and cutting into squares.
9. Enjoy these tangy and sweet Lemon Bars as a delightful dessert.

Popcorn with Cinnamon Sugar

Prep Time: 5 minutes / Air Fry Time: 8 minutes / Servings: 4 / Mode: Air Fry

Ingredients:
* 75g popcorn kernels
* 2 tablespoons coconut oil, melted
* 2 tablespoons granulated sugar
* 1 teaspoon ground cinnamon
* Pinch of salt

Preparation Instructions:
1. Preheat the air fryer to 375°F.
2. Place popcorn kernels in the air fryer basket and air fry until popped.
3. In a bowl, mix melted coconut oil, granulated sugar, ground cinnamon, and a pinch of salt.
4. Drizzle the cinnamon sugar mixture over the popped popcorn and toss to coat.
5. Air fry for an additional 3 minutes to caramelise the cinnamon sugar coating.
6. Allow the Popcorn with Cinnamon Sugar to cool slightly before serving as a delicious and aromatic snack.

Cinnamon Sugar Pretzels

Prep Time: 10 minutes / Air Fry Time: 8 minutes / Servings: 12 pretzels / Mode: Air Fry

Ingredients:
- 100g pretzel rods
- 2 tablespoons granulated sugar
- 2 tablespoons melted butter
- 1 teaspoon ground cinnamon

Preparation Instructions:
1. Preheat the air fryer to 350°F.
2. In a bowl, mix melted butter, granulated sugar, and ground cinnamon.
3. Dip each pretzel rod into the cinnamon sugar mixture, coating it evenly.
4. Place the coated pretzels in the air fryer basket, leaving space between each.
5. Air fry for 8 minutes, turning the pretzels halfway through, until they are golden and crispy.
6. Remove from the air fryer and let them cool slightly.
7. Serve these Air-Fried Cinnamon Sugar Pretzels as a delightful and quick treat.

Mini Fruit Tarts

Prep Time: 20 minutes / Cook Time: 15 minutes / Servings: 12 mini tarts / Mode: Bake

Ingredients:
- For the Tart Shells:
- 180g all-purpose flour
- 90g unsalted butter, cold and cubed
- 30g powdered sugar
- 1 egg yolk
- 1-2 tablespoons cold water
- For the Filling:
- 120g cream cheese, softened
- 60g powdered sugar
- 1 teaspoon vanilla extract
- Assorted fresh fruits (strawberries, kiwi, blueberries)

Preparation Instructions:
1. Preheat the air fryer to 350°F in Bake mode.
2. In a food processor, combine all-purpose flour, cold cubed unsalted butter, powdered sugar, and egg yolk. Pulse until the mixture resembles breadcrumbs.
3. Add cold water, one tablespoon at a time, until the dough comes together. Shape into a ball, wrap in plastic wrap, and chill for 10 minutes.
4. Roll out the chilled dough and cut into circles to fit mini tart pans. Press the dough into the pans.
5. Bake the tart shells in the air fryer for 15 minutes or until golden.
6. In a bowl, mix softened cream cheese, powdered sugar, and vanilla extract for the filling.
7. Once the tart shells are cooled, fill each with the cream cheese mixture.
8. Top with assorted fresh fruits.
9. Serve these delightful Mini Fruit Tarts as a colorful and delicious dessert.

Apple Cinnamon Oat Bars

Prep Time: 15 minutes / Cook Time: 12 minutes / Servings: 12 bars / Mode: Air Fry

Ingredients:
- 160g rolled oats
- 120g chopped dried apples
- 120g almond butter
- 80ml honey
- 60ml melted coconut oil
- 1 teaspoon ground cinnamon
- 1/2 teaspoon vanilla extract
- Pinch of salt

Preparation Instructions:
1. In a large bowl, combine rolled oats and chopped dried apples.
2. In a saucepan, heat almond butter, honey, melted coconut oil, ground cinnamon, vanilla extract, and a pinch of salt until well combined.
3. Pour the wet mixture over the dry ingredients and stir until evenly coated.
4. Press the mixture into the air fryer basket, creating an even layer.
5. Air fry at 350°F for 12 minutes, shaking the basket halfway through, until the bars are golden and set.
6. Once cooled, cut into bars and enjoy these Air-Fried Apple Cinnamon Oat Bars.

Blueberry Muffins

Prep Time: 15 minutes / Cook Time: 20 minutes / Servings: 12 muffins / Mode: Bake

Ingredients:

- 240g all-purpose flour
- 1/2 teaspoon salt
- 60ml melted butter
- 100g granulated sugar
- 150g fresh or frozen blueberries
- 1 large egg
- 1 tablespoon baking powder
- 240ml milk
- 1 teaspoon vanilla extract

Preparation Instructions:

1. Preheat the air fryer to 375°F in Bake mode.
2. In a large bowl, whisk together all-purpose flour, granulated sugar, baking powder, and salt.
3. Gently fold in blueberries.
4. In another bowl, whisk together milk, melted butter, egg, and vanilla extract.
5. Add the wet ingredients to the dry ingredients, stirring until just combined.
6. Line the muffin cups with paper liners.
7. Fill each muffin cup with the batter, about two-thirds full.
8. Bake in the air fryer for 20 minutes or until a toothpick inserted into the center comes out clean.
9. Allow the Blueberry Muffins to cool before serving as a delightful breakfast or snack.

Banana Chips with Chocolate Drizzle

Prep Time: 10 minutes / Cook Time: 8 minutes / Servings: 2 / Mode: Air Fry

Ingredients:

- 2 bananas, peeled and sliced
- 1 tablespoon chopped nuts (e.g., almonds or walnuts)
- 2 tablespoons dark chocolate, melted

Preparation Instructions:

1. Preheat the air fryer to 375°F.
2. Place banana slices in the air fryer basket.
3. Air fry for 8 minutes, shaking the basket halfway through.
4. Drizzle melted dark chocolate over the air-fried banana chips.
5. Sprinkle chopped nuts on top.
6. Serve these delicious Banana Chips with Chocolate Drizzle as a quick and tasty snack.

Almond and Coconut Bites

Prep Time: 15 minutes / Cook Time: 10 minutes / Servings: 12 bites / Mode: Air Fry

Ingredients:

- 120g almonds
- 1 tablespoon honey
- 40g shredded coconut
- 1/2 teaspoon almond extract
- 2 tablespoons almond butter

Preparation Instructions:

1. In a food processor, combine almonds, shredded coconut, almond butter, honey, and almond extract.
2. Pulse until the mixture forms a sticky dough.
3. Scoop out tablespoon-sized portions of the mixture and roll them into bites.
4. Place the bites in the air fryer basket.
5. Air fry at 350°F for 10 minutes, shaking the basket halfway through.
6. Once cooked, these Air-Fried Almond and Coconut Bites are ready to be enjoyed as a wholesome and satisfying snack.

Raspberry Cheesecake Bites

Prep Time: 15 minutes / Cook Time: 8 minutes / Servings: 12 bites / Mode: Air Fry

Ingredients:
- 120g cream cheese, softened
- 60g fresh raspberries
- 2 tablespoons sugar
- 1 sheet puff pastry, thawed
- 1/2 teaspoon vanilla extract
- Powdered sugar for dusting

Preparation Instructions:
1. In a bowl, beat together softened cream cheese, sugar, and vanilla extract until smooth.
2. Gently fold in fresh raspberries into the cream cheese mixture.
3. Roll out the puff pastry sheet and cut it into 12 squares.
4. Spoon a dollop of the raspberry cream cheese mixture onto each puff pastry square.
5. Fold the pastry over the filling, sealing the edges to form a bite-sized pocket.
6. Place the bites in the air fryer basket.
7. Air fry at 375°F for 8 minutes or until the pastry is golden and puffed.
8. Dust with powdered sugar before serving these delightful Raspberry Cheesecake Bites.

Peach Cobbler Bites

Prep Time: 15 minutes / Cook Time: 10 minutes / Servings: 12 bites / Mode: Air Fry

Ingredients:
- 150g diced peaches
- 1 sheet puff pastry, thawed
- 2 tablespoons brown sugar
- Vanilla ice cream for serving (optional)
- 1/2 teaspoon ground cinnamon

Preparation Instructions:
1. In a bowl, mix diced peaches with brown sugar and ground cinnamon.
2. Roll out the puff pastry sheet and cut it into 12 squares.
3. Spoon a portion of the peach mixture onto each puff pastry square.
4. Fold the pastry over the filling, sealing the edges.
5. Place the bites in the air fryer basket.
6. Air fry at 375°F for 10 minutes or until the pastry is golden and cooked through.
7. Serve these Peach Cobbler Bites on their own or with a scoop of vanilla ice cream if desired.

Vanilla Almond Biscotti

Prep Time: 15 minutes / Cook Time: 15 minutes / Servings: 12 biscotti / Mode: Air Fry

Ingredients:
- 120g all-purpose flour
- Pinch of salt
- 60g sliced almonds
- 100g granulated sugar
- 1 large egg
- 1/2 teaspoon baking powder
- 1 teaspoon vanilla extract

Preparation Instructions:
1. In a bowl, whisk together all-purpose flour, granulated sugar, baking powder, and a pinch of salt.
2. In a separate bowl, beat the egg and stir in vanilla extract.
3. Add the wet ingredients to the dry ingredients, mixing until a dough forms.
4. Fold in sliced almonds to evenly distribute throughout the dough.
5. Shape the dough into a log on a parchment-lined tray.
6. Air fry at 350°F for 15 minutes, turning the log halfway through.
7. Once golden and firm, remove from the air fryer and let it cool for a few minutes.
8. Slice the log into biscotti shapes and allow them to cool completely before serving.

Snickerdoodle Cookies

Prep Time: 15 minutes / Cook Time: 10 minutes / Servings: 12 cookies / Mode: Air Fry

Ingredients:
- 180g all-purpose flour
- 113g unsalted butter, softened
- 100g granulated sugar

- 1 large egg
- 1 teaspoon vanilla extract
- 1/4 teaspoon cream of tartar
- 1/4 teaspoon baking soda
- 1/4 teaspoon salt
- Coating:
- 25g granulated sugar
- 2g ground cinnamon

Preparation Instructions:

1. In a bowl, whisk together all-purpose flour, cream of tartar, baking soda, and salt.
2. In another bowl, cream together softened butter and granulated sugar until light and fluffy.
3. Beat in the egg and vanilla extract until well combined.
4. Gradually add the dry ingredients to the wet ingredients, mixing until a cookie dough forms.
5. In a small bowl, combine granulated sugar and ground cinnamon for the coating.
6. Shape the cookie dough into balls and roll each ball in the cinnamon-sugar mixture.
7. Place the coated cookie balls in the air fryer basket.
8. Air fry at 350°F for 10 minutes or until the cookies are golden and set.
9. Allow the Snickerdoodle Cookies to cool before serving.

Apple Pie Energy Bites

Prep Time: 15 minutes / Cook Time: 8 minutes / Servings: 12 bites / Mode: Air Fry

Ingredients:

- 120g dried apples
- 50g rolled oats
- 60ml almond butter
- 2 tablespoons honey
- 1/2 teaspoon cinnamon
- 1/4 teaspoon nutmeg
- Pinch of salt
- 30g chopped pecans

Preparation Instructions:

1. In a food processor, blend dried apples and rolled oats until they form a coarse mixture.
2. Add almond butter, honey, cinnamon, nutmeg, and a pinch of salt to the processor. Blend until the mixture becomes a sticky dough.
3. Transfer the dough to a bowl and fold in chopped pecans.
4. Shape the mixture into bite-sized balls.
5. Place the energy bites in the air fryer basket.
6. Air fry at 375°F for 8 minutes, shaking the basket halfway through.
7. Once cooked, let the Apple Pie Energy Bites cool before serving.

Mixed Berry Crisp

Prep Time: 15 minutes / Cook Time: 10 minutes / Servings: 4 / Mode: Air Fry

Ingredients:

- 240g mixed berries
- 1 tablespoon sugar
- 1 tablespoon cornstarch
- 50g old-fashioned oats
- 30g almond flour
- 2 tablespoons maple syrup
- 2 tablespoons melted coconut oil
- 1/2 teaspoon vanilla extract
- Pinch of salt

Preparation Instructions:

1. In a bowl, toss mixed berries with sugar and cornstarch until well coated.
2. In a separate bowl, combine old-fashioned oats, almond flour, maple syrup, melted coconut oil, vanilla extract, and a pinch of salt.
3. Spoon the berry mixture into individual ramekins or an air fryer-safe dish.
4. Sprinkle the oat topping over the berries.
5. Air fry at 375°F for 10 minutes or until the berries are bubbling, and the topping is golden.
6. Allow the Mixed Berry Crisp to cool slightly before serving.

Printed in Great Britain
by Amazon

36536080R00044